SCIENCE
FOUNDATIONS

The Big Bang

SCIENCE FOUNDATIONS

The Big Bang
Cell Theory
Electricity and Magnetism
The Expanding Universe
The Genetic Code
Germ Theory
Gravity
Heredity
Natural Selection
Planetary Motion
Plate Tectonics
Quantum Theory
Radioactivity
The Theory of Relativity

SCIENCE
FOUNDATIONS

The Big Bang

MIKE PERRICONE

CHELSEA HOUSE
PUBLISHERS
An imprint of Infobase Publishing

The Big Bang

Chelsea House
An imprint of Infobase Publishing
132 West 31st Street
New York NY 10001

Library of Congress Cataloging-in-Publication Data
Perricone, Mike, 1950–
  The big bang / Mike Perricone.
      p. cm. — (Science foundations)
  Includes bibliographical references and index.
  ISBN 978-1-60413-015-7 (hardcover)
1. Big bang theory—Juvenile literature. I. Title. II. Series.
  QB991.B54P47 2009
  523.1'8—dc22   2008047254

Chelsea House books are available at special discounts when purchased in bulk quantities for businesses, associations, institutions, or sales promotions. Please call our Special Sales Department in New York at (212) 967-8800 or (800) 322-8755.

You can find Chelsea House on the World Wide Web at
http://www.chelseahouse.com

Text design by Kerry Casey
Cover design by Ben Peterson

Printed in the United States of America

Bang EJB 10 9 8 7 6 5 4 3 2 1

This book is printed on acid-free paper.

All links and Web addresses were checked and verified to be correct at the time of publication. Because of the dynamic nature of the Web, some addresses and links may have changed since publication and may no longer be valid.

Contents

Edwin Hubble and the 20th Century Universe

The **Universe** began 13.7 billion years ago. But the concept of the Universe as we know it today—the expanding Universe of black holes, **dark matter**, and **dark energy**—is less than a hundred years old.

In the 1920s, many scientists still thought the **Milky Way** was the only **galaxy** in the cosmos. In April 1920, the National Academy of Sciences in Washington, D.C., held its "Great Debate." The question centered on those huge but indistinct, gaseous clouds in the night sky called the nebulae. The Andromeda Nebula was the most the most famous example. Were the nebulae like Andromeda part of the Milky Way? Or were they separate galaxies in a larger cosmos beyond the Milky Way?

Harlow Shapley of California's Mount Wilson Observatory championed the view that the Milky Way made up the entire Universe. Heber Curtis of California's Lick Observatory proposed a Universe that went far beyond the Milky Way. He argued that distant, cloudy nebulae like Andromeda were huge and separate galaxies. Shapley and Curtis battled to a scoreless tie. By default, the

Milky Way retained its status as the one and only big picture of what was "out there."

To most scientists of that time, the Universe was a great **constant**. The Universe had never changed; it was not changing then, and it would never change in the future. There had been no beginning, and there would be no end.

Even Albert Einstein was careful to make sure his theory of **General Relativity** lined up with what other scientists thought. His original equations told him that the Universe must either expand or contract. But he was uneasy with that result because it might have made other scientists uncomfortable. Einstein added a factor he called the **cosmological constant** to make sure his theory would predict a **steady-state**, unchanging Universe.

In other words, Einstein fudged his figures to get what he thought was the right answer. Nevertheless, Einstein's powerful ideas inspired new thinking by other scientists. New discoveries would take Einstein's ideas to new places that even he did not imagine.

American astronomer Edwin Hubble's two astonishing discoveries between 1925 and 1931 finally made Einstein change his mind, along with almost everyone else. Hubble used what was then the world's largest telescope: the 100-inch Hooker Telescope, located at Mount Wilson Observatory in southern California.

First, Hubble showed that Andromeda was not simply a cloud of gas, but a collection of individual stars that he could see clearly with the powerful new telescope. Then he showed that the stars in Andromeda were almost 10 times as far away as the farthest stars in the Milky Way. Andromeda was a separate galaxy—and it was just one of many galaxies that Hubble was able to view with the new telescope.

Next, Hubble showed that the faraway galaxies in the Universe were **receding**, or moving away from each other. They were also moving away from the Milky Way. And the farther away the galaxies were, the faster they were receding. The connection between the distance to faraway galaxies and the speed they are moving away from us is known as **Hubble's Law**.

The Universe was bigger than anyone had imagined, and it was still expanding. Hubble had shown conclusively that the Universe was a greater mystery than anyone realized. Einstein visited Hubble

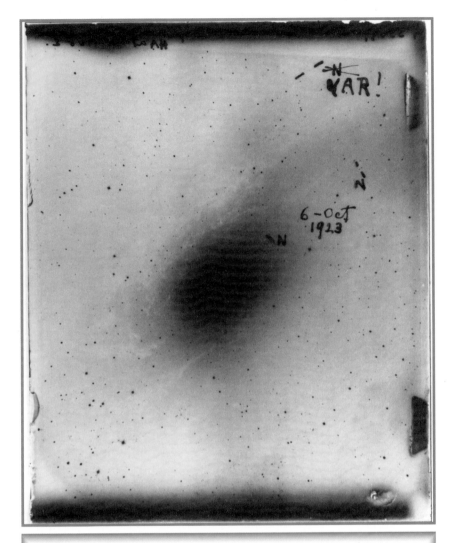

Figure 1.1 Edward Hubble took this photographic plate of the Andromeda Galaxy (Messier 31) with the Hooker telescope. It was on this plate that Hubble discovered the first Cepheid variable star in the Spiral Nebula. He at first labeled the upper-right object "N" for nova, only to realize it was a variable star, which he labeled "VAR!"

at Mount Wilson in 1931 and admitted he had been wrong about the cosmological constant. Though Einstein had resisted Hubble's ideas at first, he always loved being faced with a mystery.

"The most beautiful thing we can experience is the mysterious," Einstein wrote in his essay "The World as I See It." "It is the source of all true art and all science. He to whom this emotion is a stranger, who can no longer pause to wonder and stand rapt in awe, is as good as dead: his eyes are closed."

THE PATH OF SCIENCE

Scientists begin with the same sense of wonder as children have when discovering the world around them. Their curiosity always inspires them to ask "Why?" and "How?" They are lured by the mysterious, and they focus all their work on trying to solve the mysteries in the world as they see it—and it is hard work.

Science is not a belief system. It is not a collection of facts or a string of dates to memorize. It is not a blind acceptance of authority, no matter how great that authority figure might be. Einstein changed everyone's ideas about the world with his Theory of Relativity. He showed that time could not be separated from space, and that **matter** and **energy** were different forms of the same thing. Einstein was also challenging the greatest scientific authority of the previous three centuries: Sir Isaac Newton, who had explained the law of **gravity**.

But Newton would have approved. Newton knew he owed his own discoveries and theories to the thinking of the scientists who came before him. He once said: "I stand on the shoulders of giants."

Science is a systematic way of looking at the world and solving its mysteries. It is a rigorous method for thinking and making observations, for building a case fact by fact, using evidence in a logical way to try to solve a puzzle or unravel a mystery.

All scientists, in all fields, carry the same invaluable possession: a notebook, thoroughly and carefully recording all their scientific activities, their thinking and experimental results, even their meetings with other scientists. Whether the notebook is a handwritten journal or the newest laptop computer, no scientist is without one. The notebooks of great scientists like Edwin Hubble, Albert Einstein, and Sir Isaac Newton are treasured resources for both historians and scientists.

Scientific methods of investigating nature's mysteries have evolved since the ancient civilizations of Babylon and Egypt. Observations of the Sun, Moon, and sky were cultural and religious

The Scientific Method

Scientists like nothing better than to be surprised.

No two scientists work exactly alike; no two experiments are carried out exactly alike; and some procedures might vary from one field of science to another. But the basic steps of what is called the **scientific method** are firmly established:

1. Observe some aspect of nature with a critical and informed eye. Build some understanding of what you are going to examine and of the scientific principles you will be using.

2. Form a testable **hypothesis**, the question that you wish to answer based on your observations. Your question should be something you will be able to answer with a measurement of some kind.

3. Use your hypothesis to make a prediction. What do you expect will happen?

4. Test your prediction with an experiment, or with more observations. The test must be a fair one, where you change only one variable at a time and track the results. An experiment has three kinds of variables: *independent*, which you will change to carry out your test; *dependent*, which will show the results of changing the independent variable; and *controlled*, which will not be changed during the experiment.

(continues)

(continued)

Record your results and see if what you expected to happen is actually what happened. If not, you have to go back over steps 3 and 4 again. And again. If your prediction and your result are still not the same, that means you will have to change your thinking (the hypothesis) or your methods (the experiment). Other scientists must be able to repeat your results. (This is called being "replicable.") Other experimenters must be able to follow your procedures and verify your result. You must keep detailed and accurate records of your methods, observations, data, and results. While a theory must explain observations that have been made, it must also predict something that has not yet happened, something that can be observed or produced in another experiment.

priorities. The classical Greek philosophers adapted and expanded the learning of the Egyptians. The precise and exacting Greeks applied their keen analytical methods in observing nature. Among their "natural philosophers," Democritus (460–370 B.C.) theorized the existence of a smallest, irreducible unit of matter: the atom, or "a-tomos," the Greek term for "indivisible." (Democritus so thoroughly enjoyed his pursuit of knowledge that he was called "The Laughing Philosopher.")

When confronting the mysteries of nature, great scientific minds think alike—even when thinking thousands of years apart. The Greek scholar Eratosthenes compared the Sun's shadow in two different places, on the longest day of the year, to measure the size of the Earth. With no electronics and no sophisticated instruments, he came to within about 15% of the precise measurements of today. Edwin Hubble used a similar, disciplined way of thinking more than 2,500 years later with new measurements of the Universe that surprised everyone.

HUBBLE AND ANDROMEDA

Edwin Hubble was an outstanding high-school track and field athlete in Wheaton, Illinois. His specialty was the high jump, and he set a state record at a track meet in 1906. (Who knows? He might have been preparing for the great leap he would make in **astronomy**.) His work in the 1920s, at California's 100-inch Hooker Telescope, expanded forever the way we view the Universe.

But first, there were sidesteps. Hubble studied math and astronomy at the University of Chicago, then went to Oxford University in England as one of the original Rhodes Scholars. He studied law at Oxford, but never practiced as a lawyer. Returning to the United States, he taught high school and coached basketball in New Albany, Indiana.

Astronomy called him again, this time to the University of Chicago's Yerkes Observatory in Wisconsin. He earned his Ph.D. in 1917 by studying what he called "faint nebulae." Hubble already knew the importance of these distant cosmic clouds.

Then war intervened. Hubble served as an officer in the U.S. Army during World War I, becoming a major. In 1919, after the war ended, the new 100-inch Hooker Telescope was being completed at Mount Wilson Observatory near Pasadena, California. The famous American astronomer George Ellery Hale was looking for a young scientist to join his staff at Mount Wilson. Hale chose Edwin Hubble. From that time, our view of the Universe began to change.

The power and precision of the 100-inch telescope were gifts that Hubble used to their fullest potential. He began by studying the well-known cloud called the Andromeda Nebula. With the new telescope, he was the first to see that Andromeda was not just a fog or some cosmic mist, but a collection of individual stars.

Hubble also spotted several stars called Cepheid variables located out in the spiral arms of the Andromeda Nebula—stars that grow brighter and dimmer in a predictable period of time. These **variable stars** were well known from observations of other Cepheid variables in the Milky Way. (The North Star, Polaris, is a Cepheid variable.) Two astronomers at Harvard College Observatory,

Figure 1.2 Edwin Hubble and British scientist James Jeans sit in the observer's cage of at the 100-inch Hooker Telescope at Mount Wilson Observatory. Astronomers used photographic plates to collect light reflected from the main mirror 55 feet down.

Henrietta Swan Leavitt and Harlow Shapley, had studied the variations of these stars within the Milky Way. They had made a firm connection between the periods of Cepheid stars (how long it takes them to go from bright to dim to bright again) and the total brightness they radiate in all directions (called their absolute **luminosity**).

Once Hubble encountered variable stars in Andromeda, he could use their cycles to chart their absolute brightness. He compared measurements for what is called their **apparent brightness**, or luminosity—the brightness as recorded in the telescope's mirror. (Brightness varies with the square of distance. A light bulb 2 feet away will be four times brighter than a light bulb 4 feet away.) Hubble used the variable stars as a **standard candle**. By comparing their **relative brightness**, he would know their distance. With these standard candles, Hubble could determine the distances to the Cepheid variables in Andromeda.

In 1923, Hubble broke down the barriers of the Universe. He measured a distance of 900,000 **light years** to the Andromeda Nebula, which he knew was actually a galaxy. (A light year is the distance that **light** can travel in a year through a vacuum, about 5.8 trillion miles [9.4 trillion kilometers].)

Hubble's measurement of the distance to Andromeda was more than 10 times as great as anything that had been measured in the Milky Way. It proved that the Universe extended far beyond our own galaxy. Hubble could see thousands and thousands of clouds in the Universe, all certain to be distant galaxies, filled with innumerable stars.

An even bigger surprise was lying in wait: It turned out that Hubble was wrong. His thinking was right, but his numbers were not. Walter Baade, Hubble's student, piled statistics on top of statistics in his own research. He concluded that Andromeda was more than 2 million light years away, more than twice as far as Hubble's measurement.

Precision is invaluable in science, but so is the "big picture." Though he had gotten some numbers wrong, Hubble was creating a new portrait of the Universe.

Next, he studied the phenomenon called **redshift**, determining the speed of faraway stars by measuring how much their light has changed between the time it was emitted and the time it reaches us.

Hubble had an invaluable sidekick, with a classic work-your-way-up-from-the-bottom story. Milton Humason had been a bellboy at the lodge where visiting scientists stayed while at Mount Wilson. He became a janitor at the observatory, asking student astronomers to teach him mathematics. Hubble took Humason under his wing, and soon the two were a team. Humason was a tireless assistant

(continues on page 18)

Redshift

As a speeding police car draws closer to you, the siren sounds like it is changing pitch to a higher note, as well as getting louder. If you are lucky and this speeding police car passes you by, the siren sounds like it is changing pitch to a lower note (and getting softer).

The change in pitch is called the **Doppler effect**. The Austrian scientist Johann Christian Doppler first explained the effect in a paper in 1842. As the sound source moves toward you, the sound waves it creates are being squeezed together. The squeezing gives them a shorter **wavelength**, producing a sound higher in pitch. As the police car moves away, the sound waves are stretched, the wavelengths are

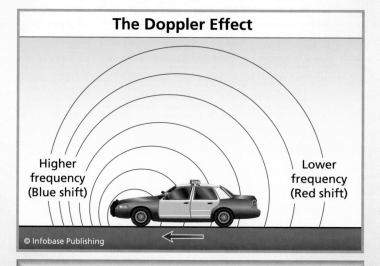

The Doppler Effect

Higher frequency (Blue shift)

Lower frequency (Red shift)

© Infobase Publishing

Figure 1.3 In Doppler shift, shorter sound wavelengths and a higher pitch are created as the police car with its blaring siren moves toward the observer. As the car moves away, the wavelengths increase and the pitch decreases. The same thing happens with light waves: As a celestial object moves away from Earth, the waves become stretched. Longer light wavelengths shift toward the red end of the spectrum. Shorter light wavelengths (as the object moves toward Earth) make the light become bluer.

lengthened, and the pitch is lowered. The faster the speed of the police car, the greater the change in the pitch of the siren that your ear registers.

Light works the same way. If a light source is moving toward you, the light waves are compressed, the wavelengths become shorter, and the light becomes bluer—the equivalent of a sound wave shifting to a higher pitch. If the light source moves away, the waves are stretched, the wavelengths become longer, and the light becomes redder—like a sound wave shifting to a lower pitch.

Astronomers use a similar principle to measure the redshift of a distant star. As a star moves farther away from the Milky Way, its light waves are stretched and the color that we see is shifted to a longer wavelength, toward the red end of the **spectrum**. The faster it recedes, the greater the shift toward red light. To help remember the colors of visible light in the electromagnetic spectrum, many use the initials ROYGBIV: red-orange-yellow-green-blue-indigo-violet. These colors are arranged from the longest wavelengths (red) to the shortest wavelengths (violet).

That police car is moving through the three dimensions that we experience in everyday space. But while we hear the sound waves differently, we cannot detect a change in the color of the flashing light on the roof at everyday speeds and distances. In fact, any color changes of this type are so infinitesimal that our eyes can never detect them.

A distant star is not moving *through* space: It is moving *with* space. The star is carried along as space itself expands. The police car is limited in how fast it can go, and even light is limited in how fast it can travel (3×10^8 meters per second). The Universe, however, makes its own rules. The expansion of the Universe might even be faster than the speed of light, though the speed of light is currently thought to be the fastest speed possible.

Scientists emphasize that redshift physics is more complicated than Doppler physics. But the concept of redshift,

(continues)

(continued)

and its similarities in the behavior of all wave motions, gave Edwin Hubble the key to his discovery of the expanding Universe.

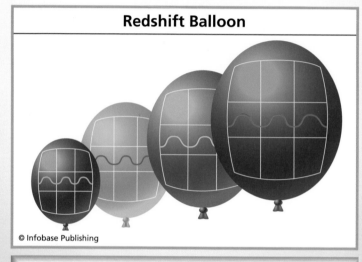

Redshift Balloon

© Infobase Publishing

Figure 1.4 Just as the surface of a spherical balloon expands, so too does the Universe expand. As the Universe expands, like a balloon, the wavelengths lengthen from blue to red on the spectrum.

(continued from page 15)

throughout the long shifts he spent helping with the telescope as he steadied the apparatus by hand during lengthy time exposures. While Hubble set about creating a catalogue of the results, measuring the distances to the clouds and galaxies, Humason recorded the images and shifts in **spectral lines**.

Sifting through the observations of 46 galaxies, Hubble discarded about half of them as unreliable. By 1929, he was sure of what he and Humason had discovered. Almost all the galaxies showed redshifts, and almost all were moving away from us. Plotting the results showed a direct connection between redshift and distance. The farthest galaxies were receding at the highest speeds.

The Universe was expanding. It was bigger today than it had been yesterday. In the future, the Universe would be even bigger. In the past, the Universe was smaller than the Universe of the present. The

Two Paths: The Priest and the Mathematician

Georges Lemaître's theory of cosmic origins created a big bang on the pages of *Popular Science Monthly* in December 1932. "Out of a single, bursting atom came all the stars and planets of our universe!" the three-page story exclaimed.

The Belgian priest and cosmologist had theorized the existence of a "primeval atom." After an unknown amount of time in a stable state, this unimaginably dense atom became unstable and began to decay or explode.

Sadly, there had been hardly any publicity for Alexander Friedmann, a Russian mathematician who had independently formulated similar theories about an expanding Universe a few years before Lemaître. After surviving both World War I and the Russian Revolution, Friedmann died of an illness in 1925 (probably typhoid fever due to the lack of public sanitation in war-torn Russia). Lemaître did not know about Friedmann's work at the time he published his own ideas two years later.

Lemaître finally did learn of Friedmann's work from Einstein at the 1927 Solvay physics conference in Brussels, Belgium (a conference that is still conducted every two years). Einstein had already criticized Friedmann's work in 1922 and was still advocating a steady-state Universe, one that did not change with time. Einstein famously told Lemaître: "Your calculations are correct, but your physics is abominable."

Lemaître and Friedmann both based their theories on mathematical solutions for Einstein's equations in general

(continues)

(continued)

relativity. Friedmann introduced the concept of a **critical density** of matter, with the strength of gravity determining different possible outcomes for the Universe. Below this critical density, the Universe would contract. Above the critical

Figure 1.5 This December 1932 article about the Big Bang Theory of Father Georges Lemaître ran in *Popular Science Monthly*.

density, the Universe would expand. At exactly the critical density, the "flat" Universe would stay the same forever.

Mass and energy are equivalent, as Einstein demonstrated. Think of a rocket launched from Earth into space. If the rocket has enough energy, it will escape the Earth's gravity and keep moving on forever (as long as nothing else stops it). If the rocket has too little energy, it will plummet back to Earth. If it has just the right amount of energy, it will enter an Earth orbit—where, in perfect conditions, it could stay forever.

Friedmann is now credited with building a mathematical base for Einstein's theory of general relativity. He died without knowing of his own success.

Lemaître was more fortunate. He had studied civil engineering before joining the Belgian Army in 1914 and serving in the artillery. After witnessing the devastation of World War I, Lemaître returned to Belgium and began his dual careers, in physics and in the Roman Catholic priesthood. He saw no duel between science and religion, saying: "There are two paths to the truth. I choose both."

simple conclusion: Looking backward to some point in the far, far past, the Universe had been extremely small, compact, and dense. Somehow, through some event—some extreme explosion unlike any explosion that was ever known—the Universe began growing. And it has never stopped.

Hubble's discovery brought observations of the cosmos up to speed with theories. The idea of an explosive origin for the cosmos looked better and better. The Belgian priest and astronomer, Father Georges Lemaître, had advocated the origin of an expanding Universe from a single "primeval atom." The Russian mathematician Alexander Friedmann had proposed an origin from a single point. Both Lemaître and Friedmann had used Einstein's theories as a starting point. Friedmann had also shown mathematically that Einstein's "fudge factor" actually might be right. Einstein's cosmological constant (represented by the Greek letter lambda, or Λ) could offer the framework for an expanding Universe, given the right **density** of mass in the cosmos. Hubble's results turned the theories of Lemaître and Friedmann into strong probabilities.

Even Einstein changed his mind after seeing Hubble's results. During a stint as a visiting professor at the California Institute of Technology, Einstein visited Hubble at Mount Wilson and put his own seal of approval on Hubble's work. He accepted the idea of the expanding Universe, dropped his own view of a steady-state Universe, and rejected his own cosmological constant—though today this self-proclaimed "blunder" has come to look like yet another stroke of genius.

Proving the Big Bang: The Cosmic Microwave Background

At about the time Edwin Hubble's discoveries were merging with early Big Bang theories, Arno Penzias was born in Munich, Germany in 1933. That year, Adolf Hitler and the Nazis had risen to power. In 1939, when he was six years old, Arno and his family were rounded up with thousands of other Jews by the Nazi government and deported to Poland. However, they ended up back in Munich when Poland closed its border. Desperate to escape, Arno Penzias's father managed to take his family to England and then on a ship to America.

The family began a new life in New York City in 1940, where Arno attended the city's public school system. Throughout high school at Brooklyn Tech, and while at college at City University of New York in Manhattan, Penzias did much of his studying while riding the subway trains to and from his home in the Bronx. He graduated, got married, and served two years in the U.S. Army Signal Corps. After completing his doctorate at Columbia University, he joined the famed Bell Telephone Laboratories in northern New Jersey. By then, scientists at Bell Labs had already captured two Nobel Prizes in Physics: one for Clinton Davisson in 1937 (for showing that an **electron** behaves as both a particle and a wave); and the other for the team of John Bardeen, Walter Brattain, and William Shockley in 1956 (for inventing the transistor). Penzias was destined to join their ranks.

PENZIAS, WILSON, AND COSMIC BACKGROUND RADIATION

In 1960, the National Aeronautics and Space Administration (NASA) launched Echo, the first communication satellite. Echo was a shiny metallic balloon about 100 feet (30 meters) in diameter. It was used to reflect telephone, radio, and television signals. Bell Labs used a large radio antenna, located at Crawford Hill, New Jersey, to communicate with Echo. With its 20-foot (6-meter) horn reflector, or dish, this antenna was so large and so sensitive that it was a natural fit to use it as a **radio telescope** for astronomical research.

A radio telescope collects **electromagnetic radiation** in the range of wavelengths called the radio spectrum. Broadcast signals for FM radio, AM radio, and TV are all part of this wide spectrum. Radio wavelengths are very long compared to other forms of **radiation**. They start at about 11.8 inches (about 30 centimeters) and extend to about 1.8 miles (3 kilometers). Radio astronomers are most interested in the range from about 0.4 inches (1 cm) to about 33 feet (10 meters).

The "dish" of a radio telescope focuses the incoming waves onto a receiving antenna. The waves are converted to digital signals and relayed to an amplifier, which makes them "louder." The diameter of the telescope must be many times larger than the wavelength of the radiation it is trying to capture.

In 1964, Arno Penzias began using this radio telescope to measure radio waves streaming from the outer edge of the Milky Way galaxy and beyond. Along with another young Bell Labs scientist, Robert W. Wilson, Penzias wanted to explore radio galaxies all across the entire sky. Striving for absolute precision, their goal was to compile the most thorough and accurate survey of radio galaxies ever created.

Penzias and Wilson tested their equipment, looking for "noise" from space and from the telescope itself, intending to filter out

Figure 2.1 Arno Penzias and Robert Wilson, winners of the 1978 Nobel Prize in Physics, stand that year in front of their microwave antenna at Bell Labs in Holmdel, New Jersey, where they discovered the cosmic microwave background in 1964.

whatever background noise they encountered from their results. They tuned their radio telescope to a wavelength of 7.35 cm (equivalent to 4,080 million cycles per second, or hertz—a measure of frequency), intending to explore a range up to 21 cm. They figured they could easily spot any external "noise" from the atmosphere because it would be originating from specific sources, in specific directions; or it would occur at specific times, such as during electrical storms.

But at 7.35 cm, they discovered a constant "hiss" that came from everywhere. And this static would not go away. It seemed to be coming from outside the Milky Way, from every direction, at all times. It remained constant over time and did not change with weather conditions or seasonal variations.

Penzias and Wilson checked their telescope. They found pigeons nesting inside and got rid of them. They took apart the telescope to find "mementos" that the pigeons had left behind, which they called "white dielectric matter." They cleaned the equipment and ran it again, but found only an insignificant drop in the mysterious hissing noise. Though baffled and discouraged, they pressed on with analyzing their data. Finally, they determined the mystery noise had an equivalent temperature of 3.5 **kelvins**, or 3.5°C above absolute zero.

Kelvins are named for the British scientist William Thomson, who was also known as Lord Kelvin. In 1848, he established a value for the temperature where all molecular motion would theoretically stop: Absolute zero was set at about -459°F (-273.15°C). The laws of thermodynamics say that a body at absolute zero cannot absorb or transmit any heat or energy.

But above absolute zero, the motions of the electrons inside any kind of body always produce radio waves. The lengths of the waves will change at different temperatures. The wavelength indicates the temperature of the body that sent out the radiation, called its "equivalent temperature." The **photons**—particles of light—that appeared as microwave radiation at a wavelength of 7.35 cm, as did the microwave radiation that Penzias and Wilson encountered with their radio telescope, would come from an object with a temperature of 3.5 kelvins.

Penzias and Wilson did not understand their discovery until after they had made a string of telephone calls. Penzias first called radio astronomer Bernard Burke of the Massachusetts Institute of Technology (MIT). Burke informed Penzias that another scientist, Ken Turner of the Carnegie Institution, had mentioned a talk given by James Peebles, a young theorist from Princeton University, at a recent meeting at John Hopkins University. Peebles had predicted that there should be radiation in the radio wavelength range left over from the early Universe. The equivalent temperature should be about 10 kelvins. Turner had heard about the measurements that Penzias and Wilson were making and suggested that they call Peebles at Princeton.

Peebles believed that radio waves would offer a "time stamp" on the early growth of the Universe. The **background radiation** would be left over from the time that the early Universe had formed hydrogen and helium. From that time, the Universe began cooking up and expanding. It began to form the nuclei of the elements heavier than hydrogen and helium. The leftover radiation could now be detected as a background radio signal, offering a record of the temperature of the Universe when the first heavy elements or metals were made. What Penzias and Wilson had discovered was the "time stamp" of a critical stage of the Universe following the Big Bang.

With their discovery, Penzias and Wilson opened a new era in **cosmology**. When they won the Nobel Prize in 1978, two other scientists were already planning the NASA space experiments that would measure the **cosmic microwave background (CMB)** with unprecedented precision. In 1992, George Smoot and John Mather used measurements taken by the COBE satellite to produce such strong evidence for the **Big Bang** that world-famous scientist Stephen Hawking called it "the most important discovery of the century, if not of all time." (Hawking is the Lucasian Professor of Mathematics at Britain's Cambridge University, the position once held by Sir Isaac Newton.) Smoot and Mather won the Nobel Prize in Physics in 2006.

ELEMENTS OF THE UNIVERSE

Hydrogen and helium, the two lightest elements, are also by far the most abundant elements in the Universe. Carbon is the "heavy" element that gives rise to life as we know it, but there is 1,000 times as much helium in the Universe as there is carbon. And there is 10,000 times as much hydrogen as there is carbon. Hydrogen and helium make up 99.99% of all the **atoms** of matter in the Universe.

Smoot and Mather: A Wake-up Call for Cosmology

Any scientist would welcome a wake-up call in the middle of the night, especially if it comes in early October, from Sweden, with the message: "You've been awarded the Nobel Prize."

George Smoot and John Mather each received those calls in October 2006. They were sharing the Nobel Prize in Physics for their work with NASA's Cosmic Background Explorer (COBE). Smoot and Mather's experiments produced extremely precise measurements of the cosmic microwave background, the most conclusive evidence for the Big Bang theory.

"In human terms," said Smoot, "it's like looking at an embryo that's a few hours old." Mather described the new information as "the accumulated trace of everything."

Smoot, Mather, and their colleagues found that the cosmic microwave background—the "afterglow" of the Big Bang—has a temperature of 2.725 kelvins (-270.275°C, or -455°F). Their measurements fit almost perfectly with predictions of the Big Bang theory.

COBE was sent into orbit 540 miles (900 km) above the Earth on a Delta rocket on November 18, 1989, the payoff for 15 years of work by scientists like Smoot, of NASA's Goddard Space Flight Center, and Mather, of the University of California at Berkeley.

After analyzing their data for three years, Smoot and Mather announced their first results in 1992. Mather led the FIRAS (Far InfraRed Absolute Spectrophotometer) experiment to analyze the cosmic microwave background's temperature and spectrum (the different wavelengths of light, like the colors of the visible spectrum). Smoot led the DMR (Differential Microwave Radiometer) experiment, which measured temperature variations within the cosmic microwave background. These ultra-tiny variations are called the **anisotropy** of the cosmic

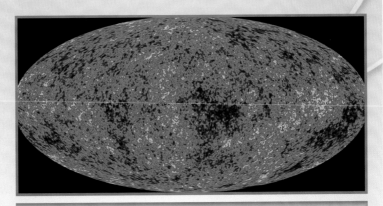

Figure 2.2   Using three years of Wilkinson Microwave Anisotropy Probe data, scientists were able to create this image of the infant universe. The color differences indicate the 13.7 billion-year-old temperature fluctuations, which correspond to the seeds of future galaxies.

microwave background. Over billions of years, however, gravity asserted its effects on these variations to produce stars, galaxies, galaxy **clusters**, and the large-scale structure of the Universe.

Smoot and Mather produced a map of the cosmic microwave background. They had a snapshot of the light released in the Universe when all the particles in the hot "primordial soup" settled into **equilibrium**, at a stable temperature. When the radiation, or energy, was first emitted, the temperature of the Universe was about 5,400°F (3,000°C). With expansion and cooling, the Universe reached the relatively stable temperature of the cosmic microwave background after 389,000 years, with a few hot and cold spots here and there.

After he received the wake-up call announcing his Nobel Prize, Mather was not sure how he might celebrate that day. Smoot, however, knew he would be extra busy: He had to finish preparing a mid-term exam for his 170 physics students at Berkeley.

Physicist George Gamow had proposed a Big Bang-type theory to explain how the nuclei of heavy atoms like carbon were formed in the early Universe. This process is called **nucleosynthesis**—the fusing of light atomic nuclei into heavier ones. In the early 1940s, Gamow proposed that the early Universe was a dense, compact soup of hydrogen nuclei (he gave it the humorous name "ylem," pronounced "EYE-lem," an obscure term he found in a dictionary). The soup expanded explosively, supplying enough energy to fuse hydrogen nuclei into helium nuclei. Hydrogen has the simplest **nucleus** of all the elements, with just one **proton**. Helium is next, with two protons and two neutral particles called **neutrons** (all particles inside the atomic nucleus are called **nucleons**).

In the hot, dense early Universe, the **fusion** that produced helium could continue, producing heavier and heavier atoms. Eventually, the pace would taper off. The slowdown would produce two permanent characteristics of the Universe: the superabundance of hydrogen and the comparative rarity of the heavier elements like carbon.

To Gamow, starting out with an all-hydrogen Universe was the most likely way to produce a Universe that was still dominated by hydrogen billions of years later. But Gamow also saw that producing helium nuclei from fusion in a star like the Sun was too slow a process to explain the makeup of the Universe. That production rate in stars, he calculated, would have taken more than 26 billion years to produce the correct proportion of helium. That was far longer than the age of the Universe (then still pegged at only 1.8 billion years, using Edwin Hubble's original, but inaccurate, estimate). Gamow thought something violent and extreme must have taken place long before the stars were formed and began manufacturing helium.

Gamow needed to know more about nuclear physics, but most of the nuclear physicists in America were cloistered in the secret Manhattan Project to build the first atomic bomb during World War II. Like Arno Penzias, Gamow was a refugee. He had fled the Soviet Union in 1933 with his wife, who was also a physicist, by way of the Solvay Conference in Brussels. Though he had been teaching at George Washington University since 1934, and the Soviets had condemned him to death for defecting, he was still regarded as a security risk and so was excluded from the Manhattan Project and cut off from access to the thinking of the best nuclear physicists of that time.

In 1945, Gamow teamed up with Ralph Alpher. A doctoral candidate at George Washington University, Alpher was brilliant in mathematics, a critical skill in the time before computers came on the scene. Alpher's calculations showed that the earliest stage of the Universe would be too hot (with temperatures in the billions of degrees Celsius) and too chaotic to allow nuclear interactions. A much later stage (with temperatures in millions of degrees Celsius) would be too cool. The just-right temperature in between had to be cooler than billions of degrees, but hotter than millions of degrees. Scientists began calling it "the Goldilocks theory."

In about three years, Gamow and Alpher produced a stunning result: The Big Bang origin of the Universe explained the formation of the two lightest elements, with 10 times as much hydrogen as helium, exactly the proportion determined through observation of the cosmos.

THE PLASMA UNIVERSE

Alpher later worked with colleague Robert Herman to explore what happened when the Universe cooled down following the era of nucleosynthesis. They found that when the Universe had cooled to a temperature of a million degrees, it was still too hot for atomic nuclei to put a lock on all of the free electrons that were passing around them. This next stage of the Universe was a hot soup called a **plasma**, the fourth state of matter. Solid, liquid, and gas are the other three states of matter.

Along with unattached nuclei and charged free electrons, Alpher and Herman said the plasma of the early Universe also contained huge numbers of photons, or particles of light. The photons, which carry no charge, would be **scattered** like fog by the charged particles. The Universe would be **opaque**: Nothing would be visible except fog, just as a car's headlights cannot penetrate a heavy fog.

Eventually, the Universe cooled enough for the hydrogen and helium nuclei to capture electrons, and thereby form complete atoms.

(continues on page 35)

Phase Transitions

When you boil a pot of water and watch the steam rise, you are seeing a key physics principle at work in the evolution of the Universe: **phase transition**, the physical change from one state of matter to another.

Matter exists in four states: solid, liquid, gas, and plasma. Boiling water demonstrates the phase transition from liquid to gas (vaporization). Water that changes from liquid to solid (ice) is freezing or solidifying. Changing from solid to liquid is called melting, or liquefaction. Changing from gas to liquid is called condensation.

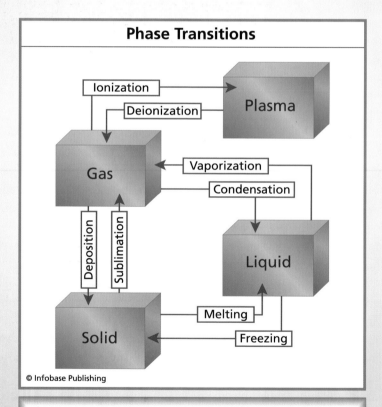

© Infobase Publishing

Figure 2.3   Phase transitions can work in both directions and even skip phases.

A rapid phase transition can skip over a state in the middle. For example, going directly from a solid to a gas is called sublimation. The reverse process—from gas directly to solid—is deposition.

In any phase transition, the key variables are temperature and pressure. Temperature measures the average kinetic energy of moving molecules (thermal energy). **Heat** is the transfer of thermal energy from one source to another.

Water is liquid between 32°F (0°C) and 212°F (100°C). Below 32°F (0°C), water freezes, a phase transition from liquid to solid as the average kinetic energy of its molecules decreases. If the temperature rises above 212°F (100°C), water vaporizes: It transitions from liquid to gas as the average kinetic energy of its molecules increases. If the temperature changes immediately from 32°F (0°C) to 212°F (100°C), water sublimates, changing directly from liquid to gas. Its molecules suddenly start hopping really, really fast.

Boiling and melting points of water and ice are given for the atmospheric pressure at sea level (14.7 pounds per square inch). However, at high altitudes with lower atmospheric pressure, water boils below 212°F (100°C). This is because water molecules do not need as much kinetic energy to overcome surface pressure as they do at sea level. The intersection of temperature and pressure at a phase transition is called the critical point of a substance.

Plasma offers the biggest challenges for scientists trying to understand the earliest conditions of the Big Bang, yet plasma is the Universe's most common state of matter.

If your high-definition TV has a plasma screen, it works like a fluorescent light bulb. An alternating electrical current going through a tube filled with an inert (chemically non-reactive) gas gets the molecules jumping, which

(continues)

(continued)

excites the electrons in the outer orbits of the atoms. As the electrons drop back into their rest state, they radiate photons, which are massless packets of light.

With extra electrons shooting around, and other electrons leaving the orbits of their atoms, the gas changes from being uniformly neutral into a collection of positive and negatively charged particles called **ions**. The phase transition from gas to plasma is called ionization. The reverse process, from plasma to gas, is called deionization or recombination. The plasma of the early Universe was incredibly hot and violent, spreading instantly in all directions. Billions of years later, you can learn about the Universe by watching science videos on your plasma HDTV.

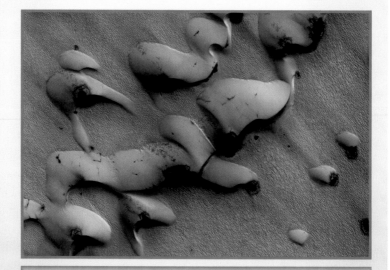

Figure 2.4 In Mars's Northern Hemisphere, sand dunes—whose smooth arcs are caused by the planet's winds—near the North Pole begin to thaw as springtime settles in. In Mars's thin atmosphere, the carbon dioxide and water ice sublime directly to gas. Thinner ice tends to sublimate first, exposing sand whose darkness absorbs warmth from the Sun, thereby encouraging faster sublimation of thicker ice.

(continued from page 31)

The photons of light were able to travel without charged particles getting in their way.

Hydrogen and helium nuclei change from plasma to atoms at 5,400°F (3,000°C). Alpher and Herman determined that the Universe would need 300,000 years to reach that temperature in order to produce this massive change of state (described as recombination). At recombination—5,400°F (3,000°C) after 300,000 years—photons could roam freely and light would appear.

Those original light waves would still be echoing around the Universe. The light waves offered a radiation snapshot from the time of recombination. The wavelength of the radiation would be stretched by the expansion of the Universe, much like the redshift of receding cosmic objects. Alpher and Herman predicted that the stretched-out wavelength of the radiation would be in the microwave range,

The Hubble Telescope: A Legacy of Discovery

The Hubble Space Telescope began the year 2007 with yet another "bang" in its career of resounding discoveries.

Using the NASA space-based telescope, astronomers measured the shapes of half a million faraway galaxies, which helped them create the first three-dimensional map of the large-scale distribution of dark matter in the Universe. A year earlier, Hubble scientists had made the first direct observation of dark matter. This mysterious "stuff" makes up nearly one-fourth of the Universe, but hides by emitting no visible light. Hubble's first dark matter observation had shown a "ring" resulting from the collision of two massive galaxies about 5 billion light years from Earth.

Dark matter's gravity slightly deflected the light from distant galaxies—light that had traveled through space

(continues)

(continued)

toward the Hubble telescope. The effect is similar to the result of Arthur Eddington's famous solar eclipse observation in 1919, which confirmed Einstein's prediction that the gravity of the Sun was strong enough to deflect the path of light from distant stars.

Hubble researchers used the small distortions of the distant galaxies' shapes to map the distribution of the dark matter that was interfering in the telescope's line of sight. Their method is called "weak **gravitational lensing**." With their 3-D map, they showed that dark matter has become increasingly "clumpy" as it collapses under gravity.

With an observation of distant **supernovae** in late 2006, Hubble scientists found evidence that the mysterious force called "dark energy" has propelled the accelerating expansion of the Universe for at least 9 billion years. Dark

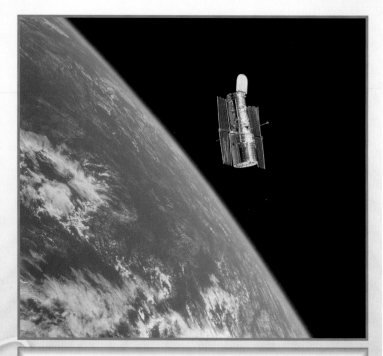

Figure 2.5 The Hubble Space Telescope

matter makes up almost three-fourths of the Universe. Normal matter makes up less than 5%. There's much more to learn, and much more for the Hubble telescope to investigate, before its mission is scheduled to end, in 2013.

The orbiting optical telescope, named for Edwin Hubble, has created a legacy of discovery since its launch in 1990. With a diameter of only about 95 inches (2.4 m), the telescope is actually smaller than the 100-inch telescope at Mount Wilson that Edwin Hubble used to discover the expansion of the Universe in 1929.

Orbiting 360 miles (580 kilometers) above the Earth, circling the globe every 97 minutes at 5 miles (8 km) a second, the Hubble telescope has virtually no atmosphere to cloud its unprecedented deep, clear views of the cosmos. The 12.5-ton space observatory has presented striking portraits of some of the farthest objects in the Universe. Hubble has transmitted nearly 500,000 images of more than 17,000 targets in space, providing enough information for scientists to write more than 3,200 scientific papers.

The telescope survived a major scare soon after its launch. A flaw was discovered in its primary mirror, but astronauts installed a set of correcting mirrors. Serious problems surfaced in 2004, but scientists convinced NASA to continue repairing the telescope to extend its lifetime.

somewhere around one millimeter. The radiation would emanate equally from all directions. The equivalent temperature would be about 5 kelvins. Detecting this microwave background radiation throughout the cosmos would offer proof for a Big Bang origin for the Universe.

And so it was that through their accidental chain of phone calls, Penzias and Wilson verified Gamow and Alpher's findings—they had found the time stamp, the cosmic microwave background. Penzias and Wilson published their results in 1965. They won the Nobel

Prize in Physics in 1978, and their work set the stage for the work of George Smoot and John Mather, who won the prize in 2006.

But Edwin Hubble, the pioneer who showed science the way toward the expanding Universe, never won a Nobel Prize. There was no Nobel category for astronomy until after Hubble's death in 1953, and the prize is never awarded posthumously. But Edwin Hubble did receive the honor of having NASA's Hubble Space Telescope named after him to carry on his legacy of discovery.

A New, Faster, Darker Universe

The climax to the twentieth-century discoveries about the nature of the Universe was among the most startling discoveries of all: a new mystery substance that seemed to dominate everything in the Universe—a force that was called dark energy.

Scientists had not yet observed dark matter directly. They knew it made up more of the Universe than the normal, observable matter that forms everything from stars and planets to tables and chairs. Now they had their hands full with dark energy, which seemed to be the largest and most influential component of the Universe by far.

For most of the twentieth century, scientists thought of gravity as dominating the Universe. Einstein's general theory of relativity had expanded Newton's laws of gravity. The famous 1919 experiment of Sir Arthur Eddington confirmed Einstein's prediction that gravity was strong enough to bend light.

THE ACCELERATING UNIVERSE

With the high redshift supernovae findings of 1998, gravity was pushed into the background. The Universe, it seemed, had been slowed down by gravity for approximately the first half of its existence. Then, at some point, dark energy overtook the force of gravity and stomped on a cosmic accelerator to kick the Universe into expanding faster and faster, possibly forever.

The revelations of this new, faster, and darker Universe first came to light during scientific presentations in November and December of 1997. Two separate international teams of researchers—one based in

Arthur Eddington's Quest

Arthur Eddington did not seem intimidated by the idea of confronting the work of the ultimate scientific authority, Sir Isaac Newton. He had already defied a powerful authority—his own government—by refusing to enter military service during World War I. Eddington claimed conscientious objector status as a Quaker, a stand that would have landed him in prison. But Britain's Astronomer Royal, Frank Dyson, pleaded Eddington's case with the government. Dyson claimed that Eddington was needed to confirm the "British" science of Newton, and to refute the "German" relativity of Einstein. Dyson's little white lie carried the day.

Though officially charged with refuting Einstein, Eddington wrote a scientific article in 1919 ("Report on the General Theory of Gravitation") that introduced Einstein's work to British readership. Eddington would eventually become famous as one of the leading authorities on general relativity, trailing behind only Einstein himself.

Eddington's first job as a scientist had been chief assistant to the Astronomer Royal at the Royal Greenwich Observatory. His duties centered on analyzing the movements of the large, near-Earth asteroid 433 Eros. The images were recorded on glass photographic plates in 1901 as part of a worldwide effort. (Eros is expected to pass within about 8 million miles of Earth in 2012.) Glass plates would eventually be replaced by film for most forms of photography. But the accuracy of their images made them useful in astronomy well into the 1990s.

Eddington had experience in using glass photographic plates to analyze observations made by telescope, a skill that was invaluable for recording and interpreting a solar the United States, the other in Australia—had spent nearly 10 years seeking to measure the expected slowdown in the expansion of the Universe. Instead, they surprised themselves and stunned the scientific community. Their results showed that the expansion of the Universe was not slowing down. Instead, it was speeding up, or accelerating.

eclipse during his 1919 eclipse expedition. Eddington hoped to observe the stars visible near the Sun's position in the sky, which is only possible during an eclipse—at all other times, the Sun's bright light obscures all nearby stars.

Eddington's expedition sailed from England in March 1919, out into the Atlantic, to the Portuguese island of Madeira. There, the expedition split into two teams. One team sailed to Brazil to observe the eclipse from a point in the Amazon jungle. Eddington's team sailed to the island of Principe off the coast of Equatorial Guinea in West Africa. Eddington hoped that with two teams, at least one of them would have clear weather for observing the eclipse.

Sure enough, Eddington's team encountered bad weather and heavy clouds, so they recorded only one usable photographic plate of the eclipse. Still, Eddington compared that plate with another from the previous January, taken from Greenwich with the same telescope he brought on the expedition. His analysis of light coming from stars positioned near the Sun in the sky showed a deflection of 1.61 arcseconds, with a margin of error of 0.3 arcseconds (an arcsecond is 1/60 of an arcminute, or 1/3600 of a degree). His result indicated that Einstein was correct—the starlight appeared to shift due to the Sun's gravitational pull on light, a result predicted by general relativity. When the other team returned from Brazil, their observations of several stars indicated a deflection of as much as 1.98 arcseconds—still showing that Einstein was correct, within the margin of error that Eddington had established.

Einstein learned of the results shortly before they were announced and described them as "joyful news." With this experimental proof, the science of cosmology joined the age of Einstein.

The 32-member Supernova Cosmology Project was based at Lawrence Berkeley Lab in California and headed by Saul Perlmutter. The 20-member High-z Supernova Search Team was led by Brian Schmidt of Australia's Mount Stromlo and Siding Spring Observatories.

Their research combined observations from three large telescopes. The Cerro Tololo Inter-American Observatory (CTIO) in Chile was used for surveying the sky. The Keck Telescope in Hawaii was used to record the spectra of the supernovae and to measure redshifts in the home galaxies of the supernovae. The Hubble Space Telescope, with greater clarity and precision than the ground-based instruments, was used to spot the most distant supernovae. To analyze the data, the U.S. group used the state-of-the-art supercomputer facilities of the National Energy Research Scientific Computing Center (NERSC), also located at the Berkeley Lab.

The two groups were observing rare cosmic events called **Type IA supernovae**. A supernova is an extremely bright exploding star that produces a burst of radiation that can last for weeks or months. A supernova by itself can be brighter than all the billions of stars in its galaxy. The Type IA supernova is a special case. Perlmutter calls it a "triggered bomb," exploding when just enough material falls onto it from a neighboring star. Type IA supernovae behave uniformly across time and space, whether near or far, and whether occurring recently or long ago in the early Universe.

The two groups of collaborators found themselves cooperating as much as competing. In total, they made up much of the global community of about 50 supernova researchers. Most of the scientists already knew each other and had a difficult time staying out of each other's way. One group would fly to Chile to use the Cerro Tololo telescope and bump into the other group as it was packing up after finishing a round of observations. Or one group might fly to Hawaii to use the Keck Telescope for supernovae spectra, while the other group was scheduled to use the telescope the following night. Perlmutter and Schmidt began checking with each other to make sure the telescopes were consistently calibrated, or standardized, to make sure that all the results had the same level of accuracy.

Weather conditions presented a constant challenge. To deal with this problem, the groups began swapping access times on the telescopes and lending each other data to guard against gaps in their observations. Each group wanted to be first and best, but neither group wanted the other to fail because of conditions beyond their control. They were partners as well as rivals.

SUPERNOVAE

Type IA supernovae brighten and fade away like fireworks, and their peak brightness is always the same. Type IA supernovae are hard to find—a "pain in the neck," as Perlmutter describes them. They may occur only two or three times in a thousand years in a galaxy. With billions of galaxies in the Universe, patience will pay off.

Brightness measurements, or magnitudes, have a long history in astronomy. Brightness varies with the square of distance. The brightness of Type IA supernovae is so consistent, they can be used as a basis of comparison to calibrate distances. They serve as standard candles. Extremely bright supernovae can be observed at extreme cosmic distances, billions of light years away. Their images are captured by telescopes with digital cameras. Spectrographs are used to analyze their different wavelengths, or colors, of light (the spectrum).

Once the peak brightness of a distant supernova is determined, this light source is measured in the same way that the brightness of a 100-watt light bulb held by someone walking away from an observer is measured: The brightness fades with the square of distance. Knowing how fast light travels helps measure how long ago a supernova explosion occurred. Perlmutter's group analyzed 42 supernovae, some of them as close as a billion light years away. They judged that the farthest ones had exploded almost 10 billion years ago. (Supernovae from different times also offer pictures of conditions during different growth stages of the Universe.)

When supernovae explode, they primarily emit blue light, which is the visible radiation with the highest frequency and shortest wavelength. In an expanding Universe, everything moves right along with that expansion—including the wavelength of light coming toward an observer. By the time the light from the supernova reaches an observer on Earth, the wavelength is stretched out, making the original bluish light turn redder and redder. How red the supernova

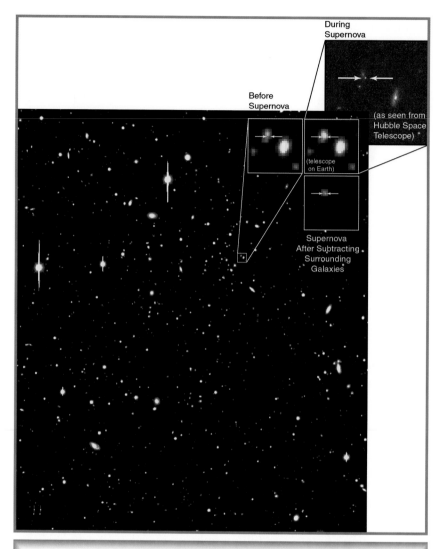

During
Supernova

Before
Supernova

(as seen from
Hubble Space
Telescope)

(telescope
on Earth)

Supernova
After Subtracting
Surrounding
Galaxies

Figure 3.1 A high-redshift supernova that was discovered by the Supernova Cosmology Project in March 1998 is seen here in before and after pictures, and in a picture from the Hubble Space Telescope.

ultimately appears—the amount of redshift—tells you how much the Universe has stretched since the light began its journey. A redshift (indicated by the letter z) of 0.1 represents about a billion light years; the supernova groups recorded redshifts of 0.8 and more, or about 8 billion light years and more.

A chart of 42 supernovae, comparing their brightness and red-shifts over varying distances, offered a map of how the Universe has stretched over its 13.7 billion-year history. As the results came in, and as the chart began taking form, the Perlmutter and Schmidt groups realized they were not getting what they expected. Instead, they had exactly what every scientist hopes for: a surprise, something completely different from what they anticipated. Their findings turned cosmology upside down.

INFLATION

Most of the matter in the Universe was expected to be conventional matter, the stuff of our everyday experience. This ordinary matter is trapped by gravity. In Einstein's general relativity equations, gravity would slow down the growth of the Universe's expansion. The more stuff or matter that was spread throughout space (the greater the density of mass), the greater the influence of gravity in slowing down the expansion. And the more stuff there is, the quicker the expansion slows down. If the mass density was great enough—if there was enough mass to produce enough gravity—then at some point, the Universe would stop expanding and begin to collapse in on itself. So went the standard assumptions.

Instead, the experimenters found that the supernovae with the highest redshifts were much dimmer than expected. The farthest supernovae were even fainter than in theoretical models of a Universe with no mass at all. Against all expectations, including their own, the supernova researchers concluded they were seeing a Universe that was speeding up, instead of one that was slowing down.

Something similar to Einstein's original cosmological constant seemed to be driving the Universe. Einstein had trashed his own idea some 60 years earlier. His intuitions told him that the Universe could either contract or expand, but he manipulated the value of a cosmological constant to produce a steady state Universe. He came to view this "fudged" cosmological constant as his biggest blunder after learning of Edwin Hubble's discovery of an expanding Universe. Yet, at least one contemporary thinker, mathematician

(continues)

Cosmological Constant: Mistake, or Another Stroke of Genius?

Bushy hair, droopy mustache, sockless shoes, mind-bending ideas, political activism: Albert Einstein always stood as the ultimate antiestablishment, antiauthority scientist. But there was one time when he strained to align

Figure 3.2 Albert Einstein and Georges Lemaître in Pasadena, Calif. in 1932, after Lemaître announced his theory about cosmic waves.

himself with the established, conventional wisdom. It led to what he termed his "biggest blunder," and it involved the biggest possible subject: the fate of the Universe.

Einstein was the genius of the "thought experiment," trusting his mind to take him exactly where science needed his ideas to go, however risky the destination.

"Lambda (Λ)," the cosmological constant, haunted Einstein's mind. It was a question with which he tried, for the only time in his career, to play it safe. General relativity had led him to a Universe that could either expand or contract. But Einstein still firmly believed in a stable, eternal, and unchanging Universe. He originated the cosmological constant to counteract gravity in his equations. He gave the constant a specific value to produce the steady-state condition that would gain the approval of other scientists.

"Once in my life," he later lamented, "I tried to be an authority."

Constants are everywhere in physics: the speed of light (c); the universal gravitational constant (G); the charge of an electron (e). Even the quirky quantum world has Planck's constant (h, the ratio of a photon's energy to its frequency). You could say that constants are a constant in science. They give us a baseline to see how quantities compare and how they depend on each other.

Einstein's cosmological constant could be a pressure counteracting gravity, or it could be a tension, counteracting the pressure of a vacuum even where there is no matter present. (A vacuum is not necessarily empty, but simply the lowest possible level of energy a system can reach.) Einstein set the value of his constant at zero to produce a static cosmic environment from his equations.

Russian mathematician Alexander Friedmann explored the full range of the constant's implications with different values. Belgian physicist and priest Father Georges Lemaître theorized that the infinite Universe must have grown from some infinitesimal (or infinitely small) source. When Edwin Hubble's observations proved the expansion of the

(continues)

(continued)

Universe, Einstein reversed field, embraced the new view, and condemned his cosmological constant as the "greatest mistake of my life." Hubble also introduced the **Hubble constant (H)**, relating the distance of a galaxy to the speed at which it is moving away from us.

Scientists increasingly credit Einstein for another stroke of genius with the cosmological constant. Scientists were surprised by the 1998 discovery that the expansion of the Universe is accelerating. They could not explain it, unless lambda really represented a previously unrecognized force, a repulsion that is driving the Universe apart, a force that dominates the Universe. Scientists named it "dark energy."

Even if Einstein thought he had blundered, science eventually showed that when it came to understanding the Universe, he was truly an Einstein from the start. It turned out that his mind experiments were taking him on the right path in the first place. He was just 75 years ahead of his time. Not bad for a blunder.

(continued)

Alexander Friedmann of the Soviet Union, showed that different values of the cosmological constant could lead to different outcomes for the Universe.

The supernovae data of 1998 suggested a Universe that was 70% energy and 30% matter. But another complex idea arose from the results. The Universe seemed to have expanded at different rates during its history. The original expansion seemed to slow down for the first half of the Universe's lifetime. Then, the Universe took off again, with the expansion accelerating to higher and higher speeds.

What was going on? Einstein's cosmological constant was a good fit with the concept, but not with the observations. Einstein's original value for the cosmological constant would produce a Universe that was 120 orders of magnitude bigger than what the supernovae results were showing (an order of magnitude is a factor of 10).

The best fit seemed to be some version of **inflation**, the theory suggested in 1979 by Alan Guth.

At the time of the Big Bang, inflation ripped space apart even faster than light could travel. But if the initial expansion were

Inflation I and II

As Alan Guth tells it, he set a personal speed record biking from his dorm room to his office at Stanford Linear Accelerator Center the morning after he had written "spectacular realization" in his notebook. On that sleepless night in

(continues)

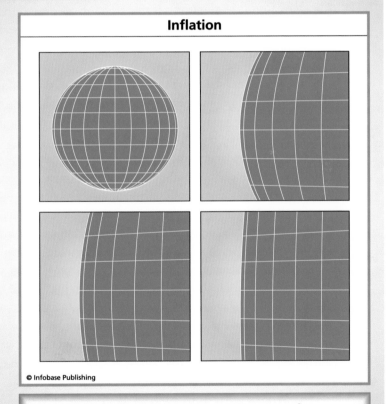

Inflation

© Infobase Publishing

Figure 3.3 A sphere expanding until it appears flat. This concept solves the flatness problem in inflationary cosmology. A sphere's surface appears flatter as the sphere enlarges.

(continued)

the fall of 1979, he was still a young researcher without a permanent job.

But the idea behind Guth's "spectacular realization" has been the model for thinking on the Big Bang origin of the Universe ever since.

Guth, now a professor at the Massachusetts Institute of Technology (MIT), called his idea "inflation." Driven by a force that acted like antigravity, the beginning Universe expanded faster than the speed of light, from subatomic scale to cosmic scale, in an unimaginably small fraction of a second. This beginning jolt of inflation created a fabric of space that would have looked the same in all directions.

Einstein's theory of general relativity predicts space that is curved. But inflation would explain why the Universe looks flat and uniform, or "homogeneous," in all directions. Uniformity was present in a tiny region before inflation began. Inflation magnified that tiny, uniform region throughout the entire Universe. The stretching of this tiny original region would make the Universe appear flat.

Inflation says that the early Universe contained an infinitesimal patch of negative pressure, which translates into positive energy. During inflation, positive energy appears as particles. Negative energy appears as gravity. The tiniest variations of density would be transformed by inflation into ripples in the fabric of space. The ripples (called **quantum fluctuations**) would grow in **intensity**. Much later, the ripples would form the large-scale structure of the Universe—the galaxies and galaxy clusters.

Inflation predicts a smoothness, or uniformity, in the Universe varying only by about one part in 100,000. That prediction is almost exactly what NASA's Cosmic Background Explorer measured in 1990. Measurements from another NASA space probe, the Wilkinson Microwave Anisotropy Probe (WMAP), charted the variations even more precisely in 2003, again backing up predictions from inflation theory.

The 1998 discovery of the **accelerating Universe** means that inflation is happening now. Dark energy has been driving this latest period of inflation, sometimes called "Inflation II," for at least the last 5 billion years. Dark energy acts like the cosmological constant. Quantum theory sometimes describes dark energy as the energy of the vacuum.

In the time since Guth first described his original idea in 1979, scientists have built many different models of the Universe based on inflation. Almost all of these models say that once inflation begins, it never completely stops: It goes on forever. In these models, not only is inflation eternal, but it also creates what some call the "multiverse."

This infinite number of "pocket Universes" covers all possible outcomes from an originating event. Our Universe would be just one of an infinite number of Universes, each with its own reality and its own laws of physics. But our Universe is the only one that we can know and observe—so far.

slowing down, the original Big Bang could not be responsible for the second **acceleration** that came billions of years later.

The experimental results beginning in 1998 suggested a second period of inflation. The current expansion of the Universe would be driven by something that was overcoming gravity by a wide margin, something that was exerting a "negative pressure" in the terms of Einstein's theory of relativity.

Some sort of energy was lurking out there, waiting in the background while closely packed matter was dominating the early Universe and while gravity acted to slow down the original rate of expansion.

The key to unlock the mystery was this: The rate of expansion had been slowing down, but the expansion had continued. Then, the expansion reached a tipping point. The density of matter dropped to a level where the mysterious "dark energy" overtook the effects of gravity, reversed the slowdown of the expansion, and stomped on the cosmic accelerator. Dark energy has maintained that acceleration for a period of nearly 8 billion years.

Figure 3.4 The most distant **quasar** ever discovered (as of October 2003) is the red dot seen here—a redshift 6.4 quasar—pictured when the universe was 800 million years old. The time it took light to travel from the quasar to Earth is about 13 billion years.

The big picture of an expanding Universe that Edwin Hubble revealed in the 1920s and 1930s had been jolted into yet a new dimension. Before long, scientists exploring high-redshift supernovae made even more startling discoveries.

Using digital photography on a telescope in Apache Point, New Mexico, scientists with the Sloan Digital Sky Survey (SDSS) announced in 2001 that they had recorded a supernova 27 billion light years away. But the Universe was less than 14 billion years old. How could the light from the supernova have been traveling for 27 billion years?

The answer was that it had not. Space had been ripped apart faster than light could travel, stretching out the wavelengths of the light from the supernova. The light had been traveling across 27 billion light years of distance—one light year is about 6 trillion miles (10 trillion km)—but had covered that distance in much less than 27 billion years.

Whatever was driving the expansion of the Universe was making its own rules of space and time. Something new was out there. Or perhaps Einstein's accepted theories of gravitation needed revising. Whatever the source, the Universe had become even bigger, and even stranger.

Cosmologist Michael Turner of the University of Chicago usually is credited with naming dark energy. Turner was also the chief scientist on the Sloan Digital Sky Survey during the discovery of the supernova that was located 27 billion light years away.

Not long after its distant supernova discovery, SDSS also found physical evidence for the existence of dark energy. SDSS is the biggest project ever put together to produce a three-dimensional "map" of the Universe. In 2003, SDSS researchers announced they had seen a "shadow" of dark energy on the cosmic microwave background—the radiation signature left over from the Big Bang.

The scientists combined their observations with data from the WMAP satellite and other experiments. They saw shadows on the microwaves caused by changes in the energy of photons that were passing through concentrations of galaxies and dark matter. The energy levels of the photons were altered by the effects of gravity. The scientists saw more photons that were gaining energy than those that were losing energy. Gravity would make the photons lose energy. But dark energy—exerting a repulsive force—would add energy to the photons. Dark energy produced the equivalent of a redshift in the microwave photons, showing yet again that the Universe was being driven apart.

The Hubble Space Telescope weighed in with its own results in 2006, using observations of redshifts. Hubble scientists found that the supernovae that were being used to measure today's expansion of space look remarkably similar to supernovae that had exploded 9 billion years ago. These ancient supernovae were being seen for the first time in 2006 by the space telescope.

The researchers concluded that dark energy had been making its presence felt for about 9 billion years—first, by slowing down the effects of gravity, the way a rolling marble will slow down if it is heading uphill; then, dark energy overtook gravity, as if the rolling marble passed a tipping point at the peak of the hill. The marble then began speeding downhill, constantly picking up speed. There is no telling when, or if, it will ever stop.

Cosmic Extremes: The Beginning of Space and Time

Here is a three-part demonstration that will help to visualize the expanding Universe:

1. With a soft-tip pen or marker, put several dots on an uninflated balloon.
2. Slowly blow up the balloon.
3. Watch the distance between the dots increase as the balloon inflates and as the surface of the balloon expands.

This is a simple illustration—but now imagine that balloon doubling in size every second. Then imagine it doubling in size every half-second. Then imagine it doubling every quarter of a second; then every eighth of a second; then every sixteenth of a second; every thirty-second of a second; every sixth-fourth of a second . . . and keep cutting in half, again and again and again, the time it takes to double the size of the balloon.

How big does the balloon get? If you double the original size of the balloon 10 times, the result is 1,024 times the original size. The balloon is not increasing in size by simple multiplication; rather, it is increasing exponentially, by what is called "powers of 2." It looks complicated when it is written 2^{10} (two to the tenth power). But the arithmetic is simple (though tedious). The exponent (10) tells you how many times the base (in this case, 2) is written down and multiplied by itself. So, 2^{10} is simply:

$$2\times2\times2\times2\times2\times2\times2\times2\times2\times2 = 1,024$$

How fast can you imagine the balloon doubling in size? The fastest pace you can imagine is nowhere near the speed that the Universe expanded with the Big Bang. The Universe doubled in size every 10^{-37} second. Put 36 zeroes to the right of a decimal point, and then the number 1 in the 37th position: That is the fraction of a second that it took the Universe to double in size after the Big Bang.

Scientific terms are given in powers of 10; this system is called scientific notation. Positive powers of 10 move to the left of a decimal point. Almost all numbers you see every day are examples of powers of 10. Any number to the (0) power is 1; any number to the (1) power is the number itself. When a number is written out, the digits or columns represent powers of 10 as we move to the left. The ones column is 10^0; the tens column is 10^1; the hundreds column is 10^2; the thousands column is 10^3; the ten thousands column is 10^4; the hundred thousands column is 10^5; and the millions column is 10^6.

Negative powers of 10 are set to the right of a decimal point. So, 10^{-37} looks like this:

$$0.0000000000000000000000000000000000001$$

By comparison, the blink of an eye (between three-tenths and four-tenths of a second) is slower than super-slow motion. In scientific notation, the blink of an eye would be written as 3×10^{-1} second, or 4×10^{-1} second. Current estimates of inflation suggest that the Universe doubled in size 100 times during the first 10^{-35} second of its existence following the Big Bang. In that unimaginably small speck of time, the size of the Universe grew 2^{100} times its original size—which comes out to about 1 followed by 30 zeroes.

THE FLATNESS PROBLEM

Many variations of inflation theory have grown since the idea was first published in 1980 by the young researcher Alan Guth, but almost all cosmologists now regard inflation as the key to what occurred as the result of the Big Bang.

Inflation proposes that the original, unimaginably rapid expansion of the Universe was propelled by a repulsive force. That force was generated by an exotic form of matter, acting like a kind of antigravity. Guth proposed that many features of our Universe could be explained by inflation, including how the Universe came to be so uniform, and why it appears to be flat.

A billiard ball is small and very round. But doubling it in size just 27 times (2^{27}) would make the billiard ball as big as the Earth, which looks flat when seen through our own, unaided eyes when we are standing on the surface itself (think especially of the far horizons in flat places like Kansas or Texas, or on the ocean).

As a surface expands, it appears to become flatter and flatter (see Figure 3.3). Every point on its surface becomes more distant from every other point. As the Universe expands, each region (or dot on your balloon) becomes more distant from every other region. But comparatively small regions—Earth, the solar system, the Milky Way galaxy—are close enough together so that gravity dominates them. The matter within these regions is held together by gravity, but the regions themselves are driven apart by dark energy. Every region becomes more distant from every other region as the Universe expands.

In the same way, any variations within a small area of space will be stretched to cosmic scales by inflation. These infinitesimal differences become the seeds for the stars and the **large scale structures** of the Universe. With the energy released from the Big Bang, the tiniest subatomic-sized imperfections were instantly stretched to cosmic sizes, like inflating a balloon to infinity, faster than the speed of light.

REENACTING THE BIG BANG

The environment of the Big Bang—the density, the temperature, the violent expansion—seems impossible to imagine. But scientists believe they have come close to duplicating the extreme conditions of the Big Bang on a small scale in the laboratory, at a particle accelerator called the **Relativistic Heavy Ion Collider (RHIC)**.

Science is very different at the extreme temperatures, pressures, and densities of environments like the RHIC—and like the earliest

Making the Primordial Soup

At Brookhaven National Laboratory, on Long Island, New York, a time machine can take scientists back to the cauldron of the Universe when it was a billionth of a second old.

This "time machine" is the Relativistic Heavy Ion Collider (RHIC), a 2.4-mile particle accelerator ring that uses

(continues)

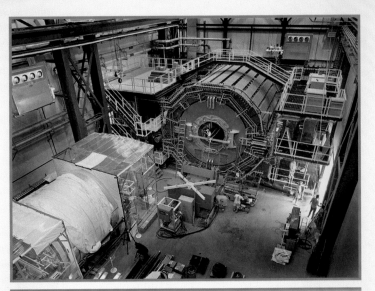

Figure 4.1 The STAR detector weighs 1,200 tons and can search for signatures of quark-gluon plasma, the form of matter that the Relativistic Heavy Ion Collider was made to create. STAR can also let scientists study the behavior of matter at high energy densities, making measurements over a great area.

(continued)

superconducting magnet technology to propel the nuclei of gold atoms at velocities within 10 miles per second of the speed of light (99.995% of 186,000 miles per second).

The dense, massive gold nuclei are composed of 197 protons and neutrons with their outer electrons removed. The nuclei then become positively charged ions. Two beams of these heavy ions travel in opposite directions, and are then kicked into collisions inside six huge particle detectors spaced around the ring.

Within minuscule regions inside the RHIC detectors, thousands of high-energy collisions each second create temperatures of approximately one trillion kelvins, some 10,000 times the temperature inside the Sun. The collision energy is about 2 TeV (trillion electron volts). An AA-sized battery produces 1.5 electron volts. The colliding subatomic particles at the RHIC are quite small compared to the scales of everyday life. The energy of 2 TeV is actually about the equivalent of two mosquitoes colliding within a space about a millionth the size of a mosquito's body. The collision region is about a trillionth of an inch wide.

The material at the center of the collision in the RHIC is hundreds of times denser than normal nuclear matter. The combination of temperature and pressure creates a phase transition, essentially "melting" the protons and neutrons of the gold nuclei.

For just a few billionths of a second, the collisions create tiny but violent quantities of the plasma, or ionized gas, similar to the plasma that existed in the first billionth of a second in the lifetime of the Universe. But in observing the RHIC results, scientists think the plasma acts more like a hot, thick, soupy liquid than the kind of gas they anticipated. They believe this bizarre soupy substance consists of fundamental subatomic particles that are never seen alone under any other conditions—particles called **quarks** and **gluons**.

In the unique conditions of this primordial soup, or "quark-gluon plasma," the subatomic particles have been freed from the bonds of the **strong force** that normally contains them within protons and neutrons. For almost the entire life of the Universe, two types, or "flavors," of quarks have always been held inescapably inside both protons and neutrons. The gluon particles act between the quarks, transmitting the strong nuclear force that works like a small, thick, tough rubber band: It stretches only so far, and no farther. But that rubber band is snapped by the pressures and temperatures of the RHIC collisions.

More than 1,200 RHIC scientists are continuing their investigations into the quark-gluon plasma. Their goal is to get closer and closer to the earliest conditions after the Big Bang.

Universe. Because of the similarities at these extremes, working with the very big and the very small can tell scientists a great deal about both ends of the scale.

Space and time began with the Big Bang about 13.7 billion years ago, and as the RHIC shows, science can attempt to duplicate conditions from the first billionth of a second.

But a billionth of a second (10^{-9} second) is not even close to the limits of science in measuring the smallest units of time. That smallest measurable interval is called **Planck time**—10^{-43} second (43 places to the right of a decimal point). Beyond that tiny measure of time, and at correspondingly tiny measurements of distance, scientists are blocked by the uncertainties created in the randomness of the quantum realm. Planck time, Planck distance, and the Planck scale are named after Max Planck. The German physicist originated the ideas in 1901 that would become known as quantum theory and **quantum mechanics**.

The Planck scale tells us how far we can go in applying science to the Big Bang. At any time earlier than 10^{-43} second, science cannot accurately measure or predict what might have happened. At any distance smaller than about 10^{-35} meter, science also has no way to accurately measure or predict what might have happened. The Planck scale serves as a starting point, connecting these very small measures of time and distance with extremely high energies and temperatures, like those that must have existed in the earliest Universe.

The Big Bang created space and time everywhere in the Universe. In the beginning, this "everywhere" was a very small, very dense

Max Planck and the Quantum Light Bulb

More than a century ago, a scientist named Max Planck set out to create an energy-saving light bulb. He succeeded in changing all of science.

Planck was a 36-year-old physics professor at the University of Berlin in 1894 when he began a research project commissioned by German electrical companies who challenged him to save energy by figuring out how to produce the maximum amount of light with the minimum amount of electricity.

Planck understood that different materials absorb light in different ways. Soot absorbs almost all the light that strikes it, and so it appears black. Glass seems to allow light to pass right through while absorbing little if any of the light. Different materials also emit radiation or light differently when they are heated.

Planck observed that energy was not emitted in a continuous and even stream, but seemed to come out in chunks, or specific finite quantities. He called these chunks quanta (from the Latin word *quantum*, which means "how much"). As the temperature increased, the chunks got bigger—again, not in a steady stream, but only in whole-number multiples of these quantities or quanta; and only when the temperature was increased by specific corresponding amounts.

In 1901, Planck defined the connection in what seemed to be very simple terms. The discrete amounts of energy (E) that could be emitted by a body were directly proportional region. The volume of the entire Universe was far less than the volume *How?* of a single atom, and smaller than the size of an individual proton. That tiny volume contained an unimaginable amount of mass, producing the most extreme density the Universe has ever experienced.

to the frequency of that radiation (v), multiplied by a constant. The constant h in Planck's equation ($E = hv$) came to be known as Planck's constant. Planck thought he was only "fudging" to make his theory agree with experimental results.

Albert Einstein believed Planck's theory also meant that light was transmitted in chunks, in quantum particles that came to be called photons. Einstein used Planck's theory to predict results from the photoelectric effect, where electrons are freed from a material bombarded with light. Einstein's predictions won him the 1921 Nobel Prize in Physics.

Planck approved of Einstein's work in relativity, but he was never comfortable with the ramifications of quantum physics (including the idea that a particle can be nowhere, or it can be in two places at once). He won the 1918 Nobel Prize for his discovery of energy quanta, but Planck called his historic equation an "act of despair."

Today, Max Planck's name is found everywhere. Germany's Max Planck Institute conducts research in virtually every field of science. The Planck constant defines energy quanta. The Planck scale defines incredibly small distances and incredibly high energies. The Planck Era, or Planck time, defines the Universe at a point so early in its evolution that only quantum principles can apply.

The Planck Project of the European Space Agency, planned for launch in 2009, aims to map the cosmic microwave background over the whole sky. The Universe itself acts like the kind of **black body** that Planck studied. Quantum theory, growing from Max Planck's quest for a better light bulb and his "act of despair," drives our understanding of the very earliest Universe.

DENSITY IN THE UNIVERSE

Today's Universe offers many examples of extreme density—great amounts of mass packed into a comparatively small volume. The Sun, for example, contains 98% of the mass of our entire solar system, or nearly 50 times the mass of all the planets combined, including the giant planets Jupiter, Saturn, and Uranus. The Sun is about 109 times the diameter of, and contains about 330,000 times as much mass as, the Earth.

Another example is a neutron star, which is the remnant of a huge star after it has exploded into a supernova. A neutron star is so dense that, on Earth, a teaspoonful of its mass would weigh a billion tons. A teaspoonful of matter from a neutron star would be equivalent to 500 million two-ton (4,000 pound) minivans.

Still another example is a black hole, an object so dense that if it had as much mass as the Earth, it would still fit into the palm of your hand (if you could actually hold it).

The beginning Universe was far more dense than any of these examples. Extreme densities also create extreme temperatures. The Sun has a surface temperature of approximately 6,000 kelvins (about 11,000°F), or about 100 times hotter than the hottest day ever experienced on Earth.

The core of the Sun is a starting place to demonstrate the extreme conditions in the Universe. At the core, pressure is about 340 times as great as the atmospheric pressure at sea level on the Earth. The core of the Sun has a temperature of about 15 million kelvins (27 million °F). Here, the atomic nuclei of hydrogen atoms fuse together to form alpha particles, which are the same as the nuclei of helium atoms. The energy produced in these fusion reactions takes about a million years to reach the surface of the Sun, where it is emitted as light and heat.

A supernova—the kind of exploding star that has been so important in discoveries about the Big Bang—is so bright that its radiation can outshine the entire galaxy surrounding it for weeks or months. Within that time, a supernova can release as much energy as the Sun will produce in 10 billion years. Its blast of radiation is produced by a runaway fusion reaction at the core of the supernova, as if the star had gone out of control. A supernova propels much or all of a star's mass outward into space in all directions, at velocities up to one-tenth of the speed of light (the speed of light is 186,000 miles per second, or 300,000 km per second).

Now cram those measurements of energy into the region of the Big Bang: an area smaller than the size of an atomic nucleus and smaller than the size of subatomic particles like the proton. The

The Four Forces

When you fall down and hit the ground, you immediately appreciate gravity's role in everything you do. Falling gives a pretty good idea of the strength of gravity as a force.

Strangely, though, gravity is by far the weakest of the four known forces in the Universe. Using the strength of gravity as a baseline, the next step up the ladder is the weak nuclear force, which is 10^{25} (or 1 followed by 25 zeroes) times as strong as gravity. The next strongest is the **electromagnetic force**, which is 10^{36} times as strong as gravity. At the top is the strong nuclear force, which is 10^{38} times as strong as gravity.

Although the strong nuclear force is about 100 times (10^2) as strong as the electromagnetic force, it can be said electromagnetism affects our lives in many ways, even more than gravity.

Turning on your computer—and every other switch in the house—shows how electromagnetism dominates our everyday experience. Electricity and magnetism, both made up of positive and negative charges, are two forms of the same force. (The Danish scientist Hans Christian Oersted discovered the unity between electricity and magnetism in 1820.)

Opposite charges attract, and like charges repel. That principle allows your TV to work when you plug it in, and it allows accelerators to propel subatomic particles at nearly the speed of light. **Particle accelerators** are used for pure scientific research about the nature of matter and energy,

(continues on page 65)

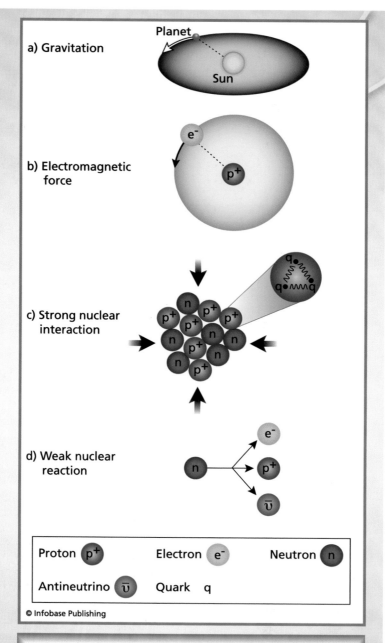

a) Gravitation

b) Electromagnetic force

c) Strong nuclear interaction

d) Weak nuclear reaction

Proton p⁺ Electron e⁻ Neutron n

Antineutrino ῡ Quark q

© Infobase Publishing

Figure 4.2 The four forces of the Universe—gravitation, the electromagnetic force, strong nuclear interaction, and weak nuclear interaction—were once unified at super-high temperatures. With falling temperatures, gravitation separated out first, followed by the next three in a process called spontaneous symmetry breaking.

(continued)

and for medical applications ranging from X-ray machines to nuclear medicine in cancer therapy.

Electromagnetism binds electrons to an atomic nucleus. Since electromagnetism is 10^{36} times as strong as gravity, the electrons within the atoms of an apple stick together when an apple falls from a tree. Gravity is not strong enough to dislodge them altogether. Electromagnetism has unlimited range, but its strength decreases with the square of distance.

The weak nuclear force has the smallest effective distance of all: 10^{-15} centimeters, about the diameter of an atomic nucleus (to compare, a human hair is about as wide as 1 million atoms of carbon). However, the strong force has a range of 10^{-13} cm, more than 100 times the distance of the weak force; the strong force is also more than 100 times as strong as the weak force. The strong force binds together the elementary particles called quarks, which make up protons and neutrons to form the atomic nucleus. The weak force creates the radioactive decay of the atomic nucleus in elements like uranium.

These forces are traditionally described as a "push" or a "pull," but they are actually created by **fundamental interactions**, the exchanges of subatomic particles. The strong force is carried between the **fundamental particles** called quarks by an exchange of other elementary particles called gluons. The weak force is carried by fundamental particles called the W and Z bosons. And the electromagnetic force is carried by photons, those tiny, massless messengers of light that bring you the visible part of the electromagnetic spectrum.

earliest state of the Universe is called the Quantum Gravity Era. At these highest temperatures and pressures, all four **forces** were unified and indistinguishable: the strong force, electromagnetism, the weak force, and gravity.

The superhot, super-dense quark-gluon plasma, like the one produced at the RHIC, represents the only time that the first

subatomic particles, called quarks, were free to move around indi-
vidually. Under any other conditions, quarks are locked together
by the strong force. In the ordinary matter of everyday life of the
Universe we know, quarks now are always found in groups of three.
But, in creating space and time, the Big Bang operated under its
own set of rules.

Freezings: A History of the Universe in Phases

The beginning Universe was a spontaneous place that made up its own rules, and those original improvisations have kept the Universe running for 13.7 billion years.

What happened in the first 10^{-43} second of the Universe's existence? Scientists cannot tell us yet. Their observations and measurements are blocked by the uncertainties of the quantum realm. At the quantum scale, any event produces a range of probable outcomes instead of one certain result.

THE SHAPE OF TIME AND SPACE

Random **fluctuations** dominated the era called Planck time, which is the first 10^{-43} second in the existence of the Universe. The scale then was too small—in time and distance—to apply any rules of Einstein's general theory of relativity, where gravity is the **curvature of space-time** resulting from mass.

Did time and space have any meaning before they were created in the Big Bang? So far, we cannot tell. But scientists think the

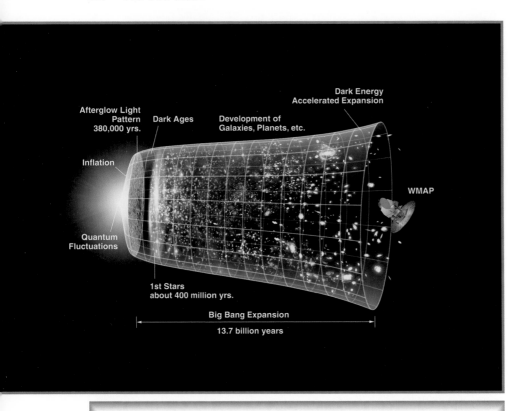

Dark Energy
Accelerated Expansion

Afterglow Light
Pattern
380,000 yrs.   **Dark Ages**   **Development of**
Galaxies, Planets, etc.

Inflation

WMAP

Quantum
Fluctuations

1st Stars
about 400 million yrs.

Big Bang Expansion

13.7 billion years

Figure 5.1   NASA's Wilkinson Microwave Anisotropy Probe provided data showing the Universe to have begun with the Big Bang 13.7 billion years ago. About 380,000 years after the Big Bang came the cosmic microwave background. This was followed by a period of darkness that lasted more than 100 million years. The first celestial objects then filled the Universe with light.

picture is fairly clear back to about 10^{-30} second after the Big Bang (0.000000000000000000000000000001 of second).

George Smoot, who shared the 2006 Nobel Prize in Physics, describes it this way: The observable Universe was then smaller than the smallest dot on your TV screen, and less time had passed than it takes for light to cross that dot.

The process called inflation took place in a small fraction of a second following the Big Bang. The Universe increased in size on the order of 10^{27} times (1,000,000,000,000,000,000,000,000,000 times) during that eyeblink of exponential expansion.

At the infinitesimal scales of the earliest Universe, quantum physics predicts fluctuations in the density of the energy of space. The tiny variations would be about 1 part in 100,000—like one molecule of impurity in 100,000 molecules of water, or one big bubble in the middle of 100,000 smaller bubbles, or one white jelly bean packed in with 100,000 black jelly beans. With inflation, those variations underwent a super expansion, along with the superexpansion of space. The variations were spread to cosmic sizes, eventually producing the stars, galaxies, and clusters of galaxies throughout the Universe.

The original ratio of the "impurities" in space —1 part in 100,000— remained the same throughout expansion. That ratio is the same as the measurements in the cosmic microwave background, the "time stamp" of the Universe about 380,000 years after the Big Bang.

EXPANSION IN THE EARLY UNIVERSE

Expansion cooled the Universe. The different stages of cooling gave rise to phase changes—transitions from one form of matter to another, from plasma to gas to liquid to solid.

There were also "super" phase changes before the appearance of matter as we know it. Plummeting temperatures resulted in a series of what are called "freezings." These phase changes in the extreme conditions at the quantum level produced the four forces. With each cooling, one of the forces was spontaneously "frozen out": the gravitational force, the strong force, the electromagnetic force, and the weak force. This series of freezings is called "spontaneous symmetry breaking." Each change added a new set of rules. As each force was frozen out, it broke with the symmetry—the uniformity—of the conditions existing under unification.

The earliest time that makes sense in scientific measurement is Planck time—10^{-43} second after the Big Bang. Big Bang cosmologists estimate that the temperature of the Universe at Planck time was 10^{32} kelvins. That's 1 followed by 32 zeroes (100,000,000, 000,000,000,000,000,000,000,000 kelvins).

Until that time and temperature, the infinitesimal Universe was ruled by one "superforce." The temperature was hot enough to produce the most massive elementary particles, perhaps even the counterparts of the fundamental particles predicted by supersymmetry. This era was the heavy particle era.

Gravity, the strong force, the electromagnetic force, and the weak force all had the same strength. Gravity was the first force to freeze off, in the first super phase change. The temperature was so high when gravity "froze out" that cosmologists still have not been able to figure out how gravity was united with all the other forces at the outset.

Once gravity froze off, the remaining three forces—the strong, the electromagnetic, and the weak—remained together in the "grand unified" era.

But the grand unity did not last long. The next freezing occurred at 10^{-38} second (38 decimal places, or 0.00000000000000000000000 000000000000001 second). The temperature plunged to 10^{27} kelvins (27 zeroes, or 1,000,000,000,000,000,000,000,000,000 kelvins).

Now the strong force froze out, and three forces were at work—gravity, the strong force, and the electroweak force, which means the weak force and the electromagnetic force were still combined. This state of the Universe lasted until 10^{-11} second after the Big Bang.

The temperature then took a big plunge, down to 10^{15} kelvins. The weak force froze out from the electromagnetic force, creating the four separate forces that we identify today—gravity, strong nuclear, weak nuclear, and electromagnetic force. This state of the Universe has been the most stable, enduring temperature changes from 10^{15} kelvins to the current 2.7 kelvins. The stability of the four forces has lasted from 10^{-11} second after the Big Bang to 13.7 billion years (13.7 x 10^9 years; or 13,700,000,000 years) and counting.

While the forces were sorting themselves out through the decreasing temperature, the enormous amounts of energy let loose by the Big Bang also began the process of settling down into matter.

Remember that energy and matter are interchangeable (which Einstein expressed with his famous equation $E=mc^2$). A small amount of matter can create enormous amounts of energy. But a great deal of energy is needed to make very small amounts of matter. Heat and radiation can be regarded as measures of energy. Temperatures following the Big Bang show the incredible amounts of energy that were available to be converted into the first bits of matter as the Universe cooled.

The early radiation flooding the Universe was probably high-energy gamma rays. These photons, far more energetic than X-ray photons, have the highest energy on the electromagnetic scale. When photons collide, the energy released creates a particle-antiparticle pair. When a corresponding particle and antiparticle collide, the **annihilation** energy can produce two photons. The chain is boundless: Photons collide to produce particles and antiparticles, which collide and annihilate to produce photons, which collide to produce particles and antiparticles, and so on.

A Timeline of Expansion

The first state of matter that scientists have been able to identify and reproduce is the quark-gluon plasma, like the "primordial soup" at the RHIC accelerator.

The time: 10^{-12} second after the Big Bang (0.000000000001 second).

The temperature: Hotter than 10^{12} kelvins (1,000,000,000,000 kelvins; about 10,000 times the temperature of the Sun).

The superhot, superdense state of matter consisted of the first particles—the quarks and gluons. In the earliest conditions, matter and **antimatter** existed in equal amounts. The beginning energy of the Universe transformed into particles of matter and antimatter. Particles colliding with their antiparticles were annihilated into energy. The plasma environment was so hot and contained so much energy that the particles were moving too fast to do anything except bounce off each other. A small number of electrons, photons, and some other light particles began appearing.

The plasma cooled and expanded. Matter began to dominate over antimatter, another spontaneous change or "broken symmetry" that altered the makeup of the Universe. The quarks and gluons slowed down enough to begin feeling the pull of the strong force between them.

In this light particle era, the Universe was too cool to produce the most massive particles, but hot enough to produce lighter particles like electrons and **positron**s. Protons and electrons combined to produce neutrons. Matter particles dominated.

The time: 10^{-4} second after the Big Bang (0.0001 second).

The temperature: 30,000 kelvins and cooling.

With the strong force binding the quarks and gluons, the parts were in place to begin building everyday, recognizable matter. The quarks and gluons tried all kinds of combinations. (Many exotic examples can be created fleetingly in particle collider experiments.) Only a combination of three quarks could form a stable, lasting structure. When three quarks became locked together, they formed a positively charged particle (the proton). When the three quarks gathered up an electron, they formed a neutral particle (the neutron). The first neutrons were free neutrons, unstable particles that are not enclosed within an atomic nucleus. They have a lifetime of about 15 minutes.

Three-quark combinations (known as **hadrons**) were the key to forming atomic nuclei. Any remaining free quarks were annihilated. No free quarks are seen anywhere in the Universe today, or in the results of high-energy particle collider experiments (so far).

The time: More than 10 seconds after the Big Bang.

The temperature: Still hot, but dropping under 10^{10} (10,000,000,000) kelvins.

Within the first 10^2 seconds, or 100 seconds, after the Big Bang, all the protons and neutrons had been formed. They began fusing together to form the first atomic nuclei. That step is called **nucleosynthesis**, literally "creating the center."

When the atomic nuclei came together, energy in the form of radiation was also "frozen out." Light and matter were separated and no longer interacted with each other. For the first time, light in the form of photons was free to roam freely. That first light is visible today as the cosmic microwave background, the time stamp of the Universe. With radiation separated from matter, this era is called the radiation era. The separation of matter and radiation is called **decoupling**.

The time: about 380,000 years after the Big Bang.

The temperature: 3,000 kelvins and still chilling. (An oxyacetylene torch, used in welding and cutting metals, also reaches a temperature of approximately 3,000 kelvins.)

A single proton forms the nucleus of a hydrogen atom, while two protons and two neutrons form the nucleus of a helium atom. Hydrogen and helium are the two most abundant elements in the Universe. Together, they make up 99.99% of all the atoms of normal matter throughout the cosmos, with hydrogen making up about 90%. Small amounts of lithium (three protons and four neutrons in the nucleus) are also formed. Now the matter era began. The process of star formation would take nearly half a billion (500,000,000) years.

The time: From 380,000 years to 10^6 (1,000,000) years.

The temperature: Cooling below 3,000 kelvins.

The time after first light inaugurated the era known as the "dark ages" of the Universe. The first light had appeared and spread, but there was no light emanating from any other source.

Below 3,000 kelvins, the first hydrogen and helium atoms formed—the atomic nuclei bonded with electrons to form atoms as we know them. Matter and radiation were no longer locked together.

With local variations in density, matter began clumping together. Pockets of gas became denser and denser. The phase change that took place can be thought of as condensation. With the Universe expanding far beyond the reach of the other forces, gravity took over. Gravity began slowing down the rate of expansion of the Universe. As matter clumped together, including clumps of dark matter, the foundation was set for the large-scale structures of the Universe: the stars, the galaxies, and the clusters of galaxies to come.

STAR FORMATION

Pockets of gas and dust formed huge clouds that were the earliest nebulae. The clouds collapsed inward as gravity pulled the dust together. Computer models predict that spinning clouds of dust may have broken up into two or three large clumps. The clumps could explain why so many stars are seen in pairs or larger groups. The cloud collapses to form a dense, hot core. Gas and dust continue to fall into this "hot spot" of gravity. Increasing temperatures and pressures create fusion reactions. Fusion produces hydrogen, then helium (which makes up more than 90% of all matter). Then star fusion

Dark Matter Candidates

From Siberia to Antarctica, from North America to Australia, scientists are conducting experiments on every continent on Earth to search for dark matter. They generally agree that any dark matter particle would interact very weakly with normal matter, making dark matter difficult to detect. Scientists believe dark matter is "cold," or relatively slow moving, with low energy.

Most theories of dark matter require the discovery of new subatomic particles. Several experiments are searching for Weakly Interacting Massive Particles (WIMPs)—particles that are leftovers from the Big Bang and have about 100 times the mass of the proton. If scientists can

Figure 5.2 The galaxy cluster 1E 0657-556, or "bullet cluster"—seen here in a composite image from 2006 from NASA's Chandra X-Ray Observatory, the Hubble Space Telescope, and the NASA Magellan spacecraft during its mission to Venus—was formed after two large clusters of galaxies collided: the Universe's most energetic event that we know of since the Big Bang. The normal matter (pink) is mainly separate from the matter in the clusters (blue), proving that nearly all matter in the clusters is dark matter.

find them, WIMPs could emerge under the theory called supersymmetry, which predicts a supermassive partner for each fundamental particle of matter that is known so far. Or WIMPs could be hidden in tiny, loop-like extra dimensions, which scientists hope to discover in high-energy accelerators like the **Large Hadron Collider**. Another theoretical particle is called the axion, a particle with much less mass than a WIMP. Other exotic theories suggest particles with even stranger names such as Q-balls, WIMP-zillas, and gravitinos.

On the MACHO (Massive Compact Halo Objects) Project at Australia's Mount Stromlo Observatory, researchers want to learn whether some significant portion of the dark matter within the halo of the Milky Way galaxy might consist of planets or brown dwarfs. Brown dwarfs are dim but massive objects that fall somewhere between the categories of stars and planets.

The idea of dark matter was first tossed around in astronomy beginning in the 1930s. The breakthrough came in the 1970s while astronomer Vera Rubin was charting the rotation of galaxies. She found that there had to be far more than the amount of visible mass present to account for the speed of rotation. Her discovery offered the most direct proof of dark matter's existence.

begins building some of the heavier metals that make up the final 1% of matter: lithium, beryllium, carbon, nitrogen, and oxygen.

A star the size of the Sun takes about 50 million years to reach maturity. The biggest stars live fast and die young, although their life span is measured in billions of years. When a star has burned all its fuel, it collapses, setting the stage for the creation of yet more stars.

Smaller stars like the Sun can become dense white dwarfs. Their intense gravity can draw off matter from nearby stars, setting off fusion reactions in their outer shell. They become brighter and begin to expel matter to form a nova. If a white dwarf explodes all the way

(continues on page 78)

Supermassive Black Holes: Gobbling Stars and Growing Galaxies?

The black hole at the center of a galaxy can swallow any star that draws too close. But scientists now believe that, on the biggest scale, this process of cosmic digestion— or maybe indigestion—can also feed the growth of stars, planets, and galaxies themselves.

The Universe is abundantly sprinkled with black holes, which are leftovers from stars that have exploded and then collapsed in on themselves. "Ordinary" black holes contain about 5 to 10 times the mass of the Sun and are compacted into extremely dense regions where gravity is strong enough to keep light from escaping.

Scientists now believe that supermassive black holes lie at the center of most or all of the hundreds of billions of galaxies in the Universe. The center of the Milky Way has a comparatively small black hole with the mass of about 4 million Suns. The Milky Way's central black hole seems to be inactive, or "dormant."

Thousands of other galaxies center on dynamic, supermassive black holes, hundreds of thousands of times the size and density of ordinary black holes. The supermassive black holes can be as large as the distance from the Sun to beyond Mars, more than 155 million miles (250 million kilometers). When they gobble up stars and other stray cosmic matter, these monster black holes spew out extremely high-energy jets of particles and radiation.

High-energy jets can be millions of light years in length. Scientists are increasingly convinced that these jets provide the mass and energy to "seed" the growth of stars and galaxies. Evidence shows that the size and violent activity of the supermassive black holes are directly connected with the growth of their surrounding galaxies. Scientists used the telescope on NASA's orbiting Galaxy Evolution Explorer in 2007 to observe the enormous flare where a star is being gobbled up by the black hole at the center of a distant galaxy.

Figure 5.3 Images like this one from the Hubble Space Telescope helped a team led by astrophysicist David Merritt of the Rochester Institute of Technology to determine how much of a "kick" black holes get when they collide. This "kick" is produced when black holes collide and a gigantic burst of gravitational radiation rams a black hole out of its galaxy, rather than creating one giant black hole. Seen here are the spiral galaxies NGC 2207 (*left*) and IC 2163 in the direction of the constellation Canis Major.

Gamma-ray jets from supermassive black holes offer a natural focus for NASA's Fermi Gamma-ray Space Telescope, which launched in 2008. The telescope will especially focus on "blazars"—jets that are traveling directly toward Earth. NASA's Hubble Space Telescope provided the first strong evidence for black holes in 1994, although the concept of a black hole first grew from Einstein's theory of general relativity in 1915.

How were supermassive black holes formed? Were they created by the explosive deaths of supermassive stars in the early Universe? Do they form when galaxies merge with smaller black holes at their center? Why are some black holes active while others—like the one at the center of the Milky Way—seem to be inactive? Why are the masses of the monster black holes so directly connected with the masses of the galaxies surrounding them? The mystery grows deeper with each new discovery.

(continued from page 75)

down to its core, it can become a supernova. The star's iron core collapses from roughly 5,000 miles (8,000 km) across to just a dozen miles within seconds.

If the core of a supernova is large enough, it collapses completely to form a **black hole**, where gravity is so strong that nothing can escape, not even light. The ultraviolent conditions in and around black holes raise havoc with gas and dust in nearby space, setting off the explosive chain of reactions leading to the formation of new stars. **Supermassive black holes** can swallow entire stars and fire off enough matter into surrounding space to feed the growth of stars, planets, and even galaxies themselves.

GALACTIC FORMATION

Galaxies and galaxy clusters could have formed in different ways. Did huge regions of the cosmos split up into smaller regions? Did gravity pull together smaller regions? Has there been a combination of both processes? The highly clustered Universe we see today is largely made up of two kinds of galaxies: elliptical galaxies, which show little rotation, have little gas left, and no longer form stars; and rotating spiral galaxies, like the Milky Way, which feature large amounts of gas and active star formation.

Gravity mediated this state of turbulence for billions of years, supervising the eruptions of stars and cosmic structures, and slowing down the initial rate of expansion of the Universe. Gravity continues to rule immense regions, which explains why the Universe is expanding but the solar system and the Earth are not. After about 5 billion years, the Universe became too big for gravity to stay in control. From somewhere, perhaps from the vacuum of the cosmos itself, dark energy kicked in, and the rate of expansion increased. The last 9 billion years pose a deep, new mystery for scientists trying to understand the Universe.

The Next Big Questions

S aul Perlmutter of Lawrence Berkeley Laboratory calls dark energy the placeholder for how much we do not know about the Universe.

Perlmutter played a major role in the 1998 discovery that revealed the accelerating expansion of the Universe. Results from the Supernova Cosmology Project, which Perlmutter headed, introduced the mystery of dark energy, the exotic component that makes up about 70% of the Universe. Dark energy has ruled the Universe for about the last 9 billion years, kicking the expansion rate into a higher gear.

DARK ENERGY

Scientists think they know what dark energy does, and how. Through a particle or a field exerting a negative pressure, dark energy dominates the Universe. Dark energy makes the Universe behave as if it were driven by something that resembles Einstein's cosmological constant. The evidence for dark energy becomes clearer with each new observation of distant cosmic objects, and with each new level of precision in measuring the properties of the cosmic microwave background.

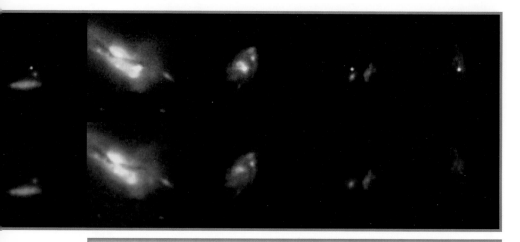

Figure 6.1 Hubble Space Telescope researchers said in 2006 that dark energy has existed in our Universe for most of the Universe's history. Researchers found that supernovae used to measure space expansion today look like the ones that exploded 9 billion years ago and are now being seen by the Hubble. This helped prove that supernovae are useful in studying cosmic expansion.

However, scientists do not know if dark energy changes with time. They are sure of only one thing: They do not know what it is. In fact, dark energy is regarded as one of the major challenges to all of science in the twenty-first century.

Dark energy could mean that Einstein was right the first time: there is a cosmological constant and its value is not zero. The existence of dark energy could mean that the understanding of gravity in Einstein's theory of general relativity needs updating, or that it could be wrong entirely.

Dark energy could lead to new thinking on cosmic **concordance**, a collection of discoveries, observations, and theories that boil down to a few widely accepted principles:

- the Universe is 13.7 billion years old;
- the cosmological constant has a value that is not zero;
- the expansion of the Universe is accelerating;
- an era of inflation followed the Big Bang; and
- dark matter dominates the matter density of the Universe.

Dark energy could mean a new and revolutionary realm of physics. It could take scientists beyond the structure of what is called the **Standard Model**, the description of fundamental particles and forces that has held up to the most vigorous testing since the 1970s.

Or dark energy could become the twenty-first century equivalent of the **ether**, the hypothetical substance that was first proposed

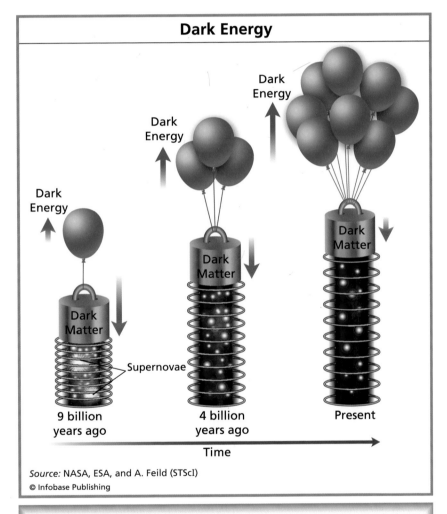

Figure 6.2 The Hubble Space Telescope found that there was dark energy in the young Universe. The tug-of-war between the pull of dark matter and the push of dark energy started 9 billion years ago, before dark energy started winning and furthering the Universe's expansion.

by the Greek philosopher Aristotle. The ether supposedly explained how light traveled through empty space. The ether was believed to fill all of space. This concept endured until the late nineteenth century. In 1887, Albert Michelson and Edward Morley performed a milestone experiment at what is now Case Western Reserve University in Cleveland. They attempted to measure the interference of light waves caused by the Earth's motion through the ether. Instead, Michelson and Morley found that any interference was so small that it could not have been caused by an "ether wind." In short, there was no ether for the Earth to move through. Their "failed experiment" set science on a pathway to Einstein's theory of special relativity in 1905.

STUDYING DARK ENERGY

In September 2006, a committee of leading scientists called the Dark Energy Task Force issued an advisory report to the U.S. Department of Energy, the National Aeronautics and Space Administration (NASA), and the National Science Foundation. Among the cosmologists on the task force was John C. Mather of Goddard Space Flight Center, who would learn a month later that he was sharing the 2006 Nobel Prize in Physics (with George Smoot of the University of California at Berkeley) for his research on the cosmic microwave background.

The Task Force stated flatly: "Most experts believe that nothing short of a revolution in our understanding of fundamental physics will be required to achieve a full understanding of the cosmic acceleration . . . the nature of dark energy ranks among the very most compelling of all outstanding problems in physical science."

The quest to understand dark energy is now driving experimental projects in the space programs of both the United States and Europe. One of them involves Saul Perlmutter, who is among the scientists working on the space-based telescope of the Supernova Acceleration Probe-Lensing for NASA (SNAP-L). Part of the Joint Dark Energy Mission of NASA and the Department of Energy, the proposed SNAP-L would begin its mission in 2011.

Like the original Supernova Cosmology Project, SNAP will use the standard candles of Type IA supernovae because of how the redshifts and distances of Type IA supernovae provide a history of the expansion of the Universe. SNAP will also use a technique called "weak gravitational lensing" to determine dark energy's effect on the distribution of matter. Gravitational lensing measures the bending of light from distant galaxies by the gravity of objects that are in front of them. The concept is similar to the technique used by Sir Arthur Eddington in 1919 to prove Einstein's theory of gravity by measuring the Sun's effect on the light of other stars.

In June 2008, NASA launched the Fermi Gamma-ray Space Telescope to observe the biggest energy sources in the Universe. The mission will use two instruments: the primary Large Area Telescope and the complementary Gamma Ray Burst Monitor to track cosmic radiation. The Fermi telescope will seek out supermassive black holes, merging neutron stars, and streams of hot gas that are moving close to the speed of light. These exotic cosmic objects generate gamma-ray radiation, which is billions of times more energetic than visible light. Project scientists will try to learn how this level of energy is produced, and what happens to the surrounding environment near these gamma-ray generators.

Astronomers will use the Fermi Gamma-ray Space Telescope to study how black holes can accelerate jets of gas outward at fantastic speeds. Particle physicists will study subatomic particles at energies far greater than those seen in ground-based particle accelerators like RHIC and the LHC. Cosmologists will gain new information about the birth and early evolution of the Universe.

The European Space Agency also planned a 2009 launch for the Planck Project. The Planck mission will map variations in the cosmic microwave background with new levels of sensitivity and resolution. It also will determine the current value of the Hubble constant, measuring the expansion rate of the Universe. It also will test inflationary models of the early Universe. The Planck telescope will use two kinds of detectors: the LFI (Low Frequency Instrument), an array of radio receivers, and the HFI (High Frequency Instrument), an array of microwave detectors.

ONGOING QUESTIONS

Exploring the how and why of the Big Bang could open up a new array of questions that may sound like the stuff of science fiction, but

Great Debate II: String Theory

The Great Debate of 1920 failed to resolve whether the Universe was bigger than the Milky Way galaxy. But the discussion uncovered the simmering questions that are about to boil over into Big Bang cosmology.

An echo of that Great Debate took place in March 2007, and it too failed to resolve another heated issue: whether the most basic ingredients of the Universe are not fundamental particles, but tiny vibrating filaments ("strings") with different energy frequencies.

This so-called "Great String Debate," conducted with abundant good humor at the National Museum of Natural History in Washington, D.C., was intended to lift the lid on simmering questions about the beginnings of everything.

Science is "on the verge of a major revolution in our understanding of the Universe and the laws that govern it," said the debate moderator, cosmologist Michael Turner of the University of Chicago.

Advocating string theory was theoretical physicist Brian Greene of Columbia University in New York. Greene's

are very real in the minds of scientists studying the origins of the Universe.

For example: Is our Universe the only Universe that exists? Could the Big Bang have produced more than one outcome? Quantum physics predicts a range of probable outcomes from any and every single event. Therefore, is our Universe one of many such results?

Is our four-dimensional Universe (three dimensions of space, one dimension of time) only a segment of a much larger Universe with many more dimensions (which is called the "multiverse")? Is our Universe like the flat image of a more complex landscape of reality? Does our **flat Universe**—a membrane, or "brane"—exist at best-selling book, *The Elegant Universe*, generated a popular miniseries on the Public Broadcasting System. (Greene is also the author of *The Fabric of the Cosmos*, another best seller.)

Opposing string theory was theoretical physicist Lawrence Krauss of Case Western University in Ohio. A prolific author, Krauss is best known for *The Physics of Star Trek*, a long-standing international best seller.

String theory, said Greene, arrives at an ultimate simplicity: ". . . although it's a highly technical subject and you can delve into the mathematical details, the basic idea is far simpler than, say, the basic ideas of relativity and quantum mechanics."

Not so, Krauss countered: "It hasn't really explained any of the things that originally we hoped it would explain. It, in fact, has gotten less and less clear as time goes on what the theory even is . . . ." Krauss expressed concerns over the lack of experimental evidence, also suggesting that string theory does not have a testable hypothesis that can lend itself to being proved or disproved by experiment—a critical requirement of the classic scientific method.

the same time as other membrane Universes? Did our Universe result from the collision of two parallel "branes"?

Did time exist before the Big Bang? Could our Universe be the current version of a series of Universes that go boom and bust in cycles? Did a Big Collapse of another Universe lead to the ultrahot, ultradense, ultra-puzzling singularity that produced the Big Bang?

And, finally, there is, perhaps, the most provocative question of all among those scientists who study the Universe, the question most likely to instigate a food fight in a research institution's cafeteria: Can all these questions be tied up with strings? Do the ultimate answers lie in the concept called "string theory"? Can string theory be proven?

The Large Hadron Collider

One of the biggest and most sophisticated scientific apparatuses in the world has the look and feel of a clean, well-lighted basement workshop: simple concrete walls and flooring, with crates of wires running overhead; lots of stark fluorescent lighting; pipes and tubes that bend and stretch everywhere; and technical components, connections, and supports that are custom made to fit into unique corners, nooks, and crannies.

But what makes this basement unique is the tunnels that run deep underground for miles. Here, thousands of scientists are doing work that cannot be conducted any-

Figure 6.3 The Large Hadron Collider is the highest-energy particle accelerator in the world. It began operating in 2008 at CERN, the European particle physics laboratory in Geneva, Switzerland. At supercold temperatures, it will investigate the fundamental nature of matter dating back to early Universe conditions.

where else in the world. Simple principles of electromagnetism are elevated by extreme speeds and energies into realms where the results of $E = mc^2$—Einstein's famous equation relating energy and matter—are demonstrated at rates of millions and millions of times a second.

At the European Organization for Nuclear Research (also known as CERN), the European **particle physics** laboratory in Geneva, the Large Hadron Collider (LHC) is housed in a 16-mile (27 km) circular tunnel, some 300 feet (90 m) underground. Positively charged protons circle the ring at velocities within a few hundreds of miles an hour of the speed of light. The particles complete the 16-mile ring about 25,000 times per second. They are focused, guided, and steered along their way by more than 1,800 magnets, weighing as much as 35 tons (32 tonnes) each.

More than 1,200 of the LHC magnets use superconducting technology. A bath of liquid helium enables them to operate at temperatures colder than outer space: 1.9 kelvins, or 1.9° Celsius above absolute zero (about −271°C). At these low temperatures, some materials lose virtually all resistance to conducting electricity.

At six points along the LHC circumference, the counter-rotating proton beams are sent crashing into each other. These collision points, or interaction regions, are surrounded by particle detectors the size of small apartment buildings, weighing thousands of tons each. The collider detectors are honeycombed with millions of pathways for digital information, all of them hand-wired by scientists, technicians, and graduate students. Their job is to track and record the results of the particle collisions. At the LHC, this amounts to almost a billion collisions per second. Each of these collisions brings scientists one step closer to unlocking the secrets of the early Universe.

STRING THEORY

String theorists propose the ultimate connection between the very small (fundamental particles on the subatomic scale) and the very large (structures of the Universe on the cosmic scale). String theorists think their idea can unify quantum theory (which involves interactions on the smallest scale) with gravity (which involves interactions on the largest scale).

In string theory, the most fundamental components of matter are not point-like subatomic particles. The particles themselves arise from the vibrations of tiny strings. These one-dimensional **strings** act like the strings on a guitar: Their length determines the frequency of their vibration. On any given string, the longest length has the lowest frequency and the lowest pitch. As the fingers of the guitarist shorten the string, the frequency of the vibration increases. Energy increases with frequency. The sound of the string increases in pitch.

String theorists reason that if the length of the string decreases to the subatomic scale, quantum rules take over from gravity and general relativity. A string would follow different rules at different lengths and would unify quantum physics with gravity.

A quantum string is like a line, but with only one dimension: length. It has no mass. Theorists say that quantum mechanics imposes a limit on how short strings can be. That lower limit on length is 10^{-34} meters, which approaches the Planck length of 10^{-35} meters. The best shot that scientists have at exploring that scale is with the new particle accelerator in Europe called the Large Hadron Collider (LHC).

The high collision energies of the LHC also will help scientists solve two more puzzles of the early Universe: Can they detect supersymmetry, a supersized twin for each known fundamental particle at high energies? And what happened to the antimatter?

At the Planck length, gravity and quantum mechanics can work in similar ways. At the minimum length of a string (still 10 times greater than the Planck length), theorists propose some unusual properties for this one-dimensional, vibrating, fundamental unit of matter.

At quantum lengths, strings would alter the basic relationships in everyday nature. The electrical charge between two particles might not have a simple and unchanging connection with the distance between them. Theorists also propose that strings would generate extra dimensions, with as many as 11 dimensions of space and time.

On the biggest scales, cosmic strings would show linear flaws in the fabric of **space-time.** Arising from the earliest phase transitions, cosmic strings would be about the diameter of a proton (on the

What Happened to the Antimatter?

Your image in a mirror does everything you do in reverse: When you move your right hand, your mirror image moves its left hand. Move your head to your right, and your mirror image moves its head to its own left. Touch your mirror image, and the image touches you at the same point.

Both you and your mirror image will survive making contact, but if you were made of matter while your mirror image were made of antimatter, touching your antimatter image would not be safe at all. You would destroy each other immediately; it would be like having an evil twin who is intent on bringing both of you down.

You are part of a Universe made of matter because at some early point, there were not enough evil twins to go around. There was not enough antimatter to annihilate all the corresponding particles of matter. It is not that science regards particles as good and antiparticles as evil. Even if you encountered someone else's anti-self, you might get along fine for a little while. There are some forms of matter—called mesons—that behave this way.

But if you ever meet up with an anti-you, both of you would be annihilated. Matter particles and their corresponding antimatter particles immediately destroy each other when they collide.

Antiparticles have the same mass as their corresponding particles, but carry the opposite charge. The positron (antielectron) has the same mass as its matter counterpart,

(continues)

(continued)

the electron, but the positron has a positive charge and the electron has a negative charge. The same is true of a proton (positive charge) and antiproton (negative charge).

Figure 6.4 This cloud chamber image taken by Carl Anderson shows his discovery of the positron. Anderson took the photo on top of Pike's Peak in Colorado. In the photo, a cosmic ray interacting with the cloud chamber wall has produced three electrons (bending to the left in the chamber's magnetic field) and three positrons (bending to the right).

That difference in charge was the key in the discovery of antimatter in 1932 by Carl Anderson at Cal Tech (California Institute of Technology). He was observing cosmic rays when he noticed something strange in his cloud chamber. The cloud chamber is a detector tank filled with water vapor that is chilled below freezing temperatures, but kept under pressure to prevent a phase transition to liquid or solid. The cloud chamber is surrounded by an intense magnetic field, which will bend the paths of particles in different directions depending on their charge and their mass.

Anderson was surprised to see particles bent to the same degree as electrons by the magnetic field, but in the opposite direction. The paths were mirror images of the electrons. They represented equal mass but an opposite charge. Anderson called them positrons.

Anderson shared the 1936 Nobel Prize in Physics with Victor Hess, who had discovered the presence of cosmic rays in the Earth's atmosphere by taking measurements in a daring series of nighttime, high-altitude balloon flights between 1911 and 1913. While Hess waited more than 20 years before his recognition with the Nobel Prize, Anderson actually received his prize before he was made a full professor at Cal Tech—the only time that has ever happened.

order of 10^{-15} meter), with indefinite length and gargantuan mass. A cosmic string just a mile long (1.6 kilometers) could have enough mass to exert a force of gravity equal to that of the Earth.

String theorists say these fundamental filaments could offer answers about what happened before the Big Bang and why. There are two basic string-related theories on the origin of the Universe: a pre-Big Bang theory, and a cyclical Big Bang theory.

In the pre-Big Bang theory, the Universe before the Big Bang is a mirror image through time of the Universe after the Big Bang. Time flows equally well in each direction, forward and backward. Events on each side of the dividing point move in the opposite order. An expanding Universe after the Big Bang is a reflection of a collapsing Universe before the Big Bang. An infinite future reflects an infinite past. In this view, a previous Universe or part of a Universe collapsed into a black hole. But the temperature and density of all the collapsed matter inside the black hole reached the limits allowed by strings. The strings were compressed like springs. They bounced back with enough energy to send matter out of the black hole and on its way to a new, expanding Universe.

The cyclical theory is also called the *ekpyrotic* theory (from the Greek term for "conflagration," or "out of fire"). In this theory, many membranes, or "branes," exist in a higher-dimensional space. The branes exert an attractive force on each other, and our Universe would be the result of a collision between two branes. At some point,

Figure 6.5 The Hubble Space Telescope captured this photo of the Orion Nebula in one of the most detailed astronomical images ever. The more than 3,000 different stars in this image are located in a dust-and-gas stellar nursery.

the attractive force between the branes would stop them from flying apart and start them rushing back toward each other, headed for another collision. The process keeps repeating itself, with cycles of collision, expansion, and collapse.

For now, most cosmologists think that time and space began with the Big Bang, but their minds can always be changed by new discoveries. A century ago, Einstein began changing the minds of scientists about how the Universe worked with his theories of special and general relativity. Hubble changed scientific minds with his discoveries showing that the Universe extended far beyond the bounds of the Milky Way, and was expanding even beyond the bounds of the imagination. Penzias and Wilson—and later, Smoot and Mather— changed scientific thinking by discovering the existence of the cosmic microwave background and showing how it pointed back toward the Big Bang. Perlmutter and Schmidt and their colleagues changed everyone's view of the Universe with their supernovae discoveries, showing that the expansion of the Universe has been speeding up for billions of years. Dark energy and string theory could radically change the minds of scientists yet again.

In the study of our universe, as in all science, new ideas, new discoveries, and new questions all share one common quality: They rest in the hands and minds of the next generation of scientists.

Glossary

Accelerating Universe   Expansion is speeding up over time, rather than slowing under the influence of gravity.

Acceleration   Rate of change of velocity per unit of time, in either speed or direction.

Anisotropy   Variance or fluctuation. In cosmology, anisotropies refer to differences in temperature of the cosmic microwave background in different directions.

Annihilation   When a particle meets its corresponding antiparticle, both disappear. The resulting energy could appear as a different particle and its antiparticle (and their energies).

Antimatter   Matter made up of elementary particles whose masses are identical to their normal-matter counterparts but whose other properties, such as electric charge, are reversed.

Apparent brightness   The brightness of an object as it appears without taking distance into account. For example, the Sun appears to be the brightest object in the sky, but is really dimmer (meaning it has less intrinsic luminosity) than many other stars.

Astronomy   The study of the Universe by observing celestial bodies and analyzing their positions, dimensions, composition, and evolution.

Atoms   The smallest units of matter that possess chemical properties. All atoms have the same basic structure: a nucleus that contains positively charged protons with an equal number of negatively charged electrons that orbit around it.

Background radiation   Radiation that fills all space. For example, the cosmic microwave background radiation from the early, hot Universe is visible today throughout the Universe.

Big Bang   The violent cosmic explosion of an incredibly small amount of matter that was at high temperature and density about 13.7 billion years ago.

Black body   A body that absorbs all light. At normal temperatures, it would appear black, but as it heats up, it emits a distinct spectrum of thermal radiation based only on its temperature.

Black hole   A region of space where gravity is so powerful that nothing can escape after having fallen past the event horizon, the boundary surrounding a black hole.

Cluster   A group of galaxies held together by the force of gravity.

Concordance   The consensus view of the Universe, including: Its age is 13.7 billion years; it began with the Big Bang, followed by a period of inflation; the expansion of the Universe is accelerating; dark matter dominates the matter density of the Universe; and dark energy gives rise to the accelerating expansion.

Constant   A factor or quantity that is invariable in certain relationships.

Cosmic microwave background (CMB)   Radiation filling the entire Universe, left over from about 380,000 years after the Big Bang, when the hot, dense plasma cooled with the expansion of space.

Cosmological constant (Λ)   The amount of energy per unit volume of the smooth vacuum. Einstein used the term in his equations to counteract the attraction caused by gravity at large scales. He wanted to preserve the idea of the static Universe. He would later regret this move, calling it his "greatest blunder."

Cosmology   The scientific study of the origin, evolution, and fate of the Universe.

Critical density   The mass-density ratio of the Universe that stops the expansion of space. Critical density is the dividing line between models of the Universe that expand forever ("open models"), and those that collapse ("closed models").

Curvature of space-time   The distortion of space and time by the presence of matter, according to Einstein's theory of general relativity.

Dark energy   The force or energy proposed by cosmologists to explain the acceleration of the expansion of the Universe. Dark energy is currently detectable only through its gravitational effects.

Dark matter   Matter that emits no observable radiation, but is detected through its gravitational effects.

Decoupling   To stop interacting. The separation of radiation from matter is called a decoupling.

Density   The amount of a substance per unit of volume.

Doppler effect   The apparent change in frequency of a wave due to the relative motion of the source and the observer.

Electromagnetic force   The fundamental force that binds electrons to atoms and governs the physics of light.

Electromagnetic radiation   Radio waves, microwaves, infrared light, visible light, ultraviolet light, X-rays, and gamma rays.

Electron   A negatively charged elementary particle that usually resides outside the nucleus of an atom, but is bound to it by electromagnetic force.

Energy   A system's ability to perform work. Mass and energy are interchangeable through Einstein's famous equation $E = mc^2$.

Equilibrium   A state of perfect balance. As long as a system is untouched by external forces, it remains in balance. All systems naturally fall toward a state of equilibrium.

Ether   A hypothetical substance first proposed by the Greek philosopher Aristotle to explain how light traveled through empty space. The concept endured until the late nineteenth century.

Flat Universe   A model of the Universe where space is not curved, but is instead geometrically flat. In a flat Universe, the total energy density (or amount of energy per unit volume) equals the critical density ($\Lambda = 1$).

Flatness problem   Under the influence of gravity, any non-flat area should quickly get larger. A closed Universe should collapse, while an open Universe should expand so that no two objects are near one another. The flatness problem asks why the Universe is balanced between these two extremes.

Fluctuation   A variation in quantity from the average.

Force   An exchange of subatomic particles that causes the acceleration of mass, which looks like a push or a pull. There are four known forces: gravitational, strong, weak, and electromagnetic. Einstein showed that gravity is the distortion in space and time caused by mass.

Fundamental interactions   The strong, electromagnetic, weak, and gravitational interactions, or forces.

Fundamental particles   The smallest and most basic constituents of matter that transmit the fundamental interactions. All other known particles are made up of these fundamental particles.

Fusion   The process by which two or more nuclei of low atomic number fuse together to form a heavier nucleus with a release of energy.

Galaxy   A cluster of billions of stars, gas, and dust held together by gravity. Galaxies come in a variety of shapes (elliptical, spiral, etc.) and sizes.

General relativity   Einstein's theory that gravity causes space and time ("space-time") to curve, as a bowling ball would deform (curve) a rubber sheet. Additionally, a moving clock will tick more slowly than a stationary clock, but only at the high velocities approaching the speed of light.

Gluon   An elementary particle that enables the interaction of quarks, as well the binding of protons and neutrons together in atomic nuclei via the strong force.

Gravitational lensing   The distortion of an image due to a very massive object. Light from a distant source can be bent around the object, allowing us to see behind it.

Gravity   The attraction between all bodies with mass.

Hadron   A subatomic particle, such as a proton and a neutron, made up of quarks. All hadrons interact via the strong force and are subject to gravity. Charged hadrons are influenced by electromagnetic forces.

Heat Energy transmitted from one body or system to another through a difference in temperature.

Hubble constant (H_0) The present expansion rate of the Universe, named after Edwin Hubble, who discovered that the redshifts of galaxies are directly proportional to their distance from the Milky Way. Current techniques measure the Hubble constant to be approximately between 70 and 80 kilometers per second per megaparsec (a megaparsec is equal to 3.26×10^6 light years).

Hubble's Law States that the redshift in light coming from distant galaxies is proportional to their distance from the Earth. Hubble's Law was among the first observational evidence for the Big Bang.

Hypothesis An explanation based on limited evidence. It is the starting point for further investigation by the scientific method.

Inflation Rapid, accelerating expansion of the early Universe. Inflation helps explain why the Universe appears flat.

Intensity The energy moving through a region of area per unit of time. Intensity is proportional to the light's photon density (the number of photons per square meter).

Intrinsic luminosity The amount of energy actually emitted into space by an object, as opposed to how bright the object appears from Earth.

Ion An atom or molecule with a positive or negative electric charge, resulting from a loss or gain of electrons.

Kelvin The base unit in scientific measurements of temperature. The coldest possible temperature of anything is 0 kelvin, which corresponds to -273 degrees on the Celsius scale.

Large Hadron Collider (LHC) The world's most powerful particle accelerator, located in Geneva, Switzerland.

Large scale structures Galaxies, galaxy clusters, and galaxy superclusters.

Light Electromagnetic radiation, usually referring to wavelengths within the visible part of the electromagnetic spectrum.

Light year The distance light travels in a year, about 5,900,000,000,000 miles (approximately 9.5 trillion kilometers). A light-year is approximately 63,000 times as long as the distance from the Earth to the Sun.

Luminosity   The total energy released by an object that emits light (for example, a star), per unit of time. The luminosity of most stars is dependent on their mass.

Matter   Objects made of atoms and molecules that occupy space and possess mass.

Milky Way   Our home galaxy. The Milky Way is a large spiral galaxy, about 100,000 light years across, with a total mass of about 10^{12} solar masses, containing 200 billion to 400 billion stars.

Neutron   A subatomic particle with zero electric charge, found in the nucleus.

Nucleon   A proton or neutron. It refers to either of the baryons that makes up an atomic nucleus.

Nucleosynthesis   The process that makes bigger atoms out of subatomic particles and smaller atoms. Also called fusion, it occurs in the intense heat of stars or thermonuclear explosions.

Nucleus   The small, positively charged center of an atom. The nucleus is 100,000 times smaller than the atom as a whole, but contains nearly 100% of the atom's mass. The nucleus is composed of protons and neutrons.

Opaque   Cannot be seen through. When light is absorbed or scattered many times by an object, we can only see the object and nothing behind it.

Particle accelerators   Machines used to propel particles to high speeds. They use electric fields to contain and accelerate charged particles.

Particle physics   The study of fundamental particles (such as quarks) and their fundamental interactions (four forces).

Phase transition   Change from one state of matter to another.

Photon   An elementary particle that makes up electromagnetic radiation (including light). A photon is a particle, but it is also a wave. It has a wavelength and frequency like any other wave. A photon has no mass.

Planck time/length   The shortest possible units of time and length. A Planck time is about 5.4×10^{-44} second, and a Planck length is about 1.6×10^{-35} meter. At any smaller time or length, our current understanding of physics would break down.

Plasma   A state of matter composed of free charged particles. Plasma, such as fire, stars, or lightning, consists of high energy ions and electrons. A gas becomes a plasma, or ionized gas, when electrons have enough energy to escape from their atoms.

Positrons   Antiparticles of the electron. They carry a charge exactly opposite that of an electron.

Proton   A subatomic particle found in the nucleus with a positive electric charge. The number of protons in an atom determines its element. It is a baryon that consists of two up quarks and one down quark (held together by gluons).

Quantum fluctuations   Tiny, temporary changes in the energy of a vacuum.

Quantum mechanics   A theory of physics that applies to systems on extremely small, or subatomic, scales. Quantum mechanics describes the "fuzziness" of the Universe, predicting only the probability that an event will happen.

Quark   A fundamental particle that interacts through the strong force. Quarks are the basic building blocks of hadrons (protons, neutrons, and mesons).

Quasar   Short for QUASi-stellAR radio source. It is the nucleus of a young galaxy powered by a supermassive black hole. The brightest known quasar is more than one hundred times as bright as our entire galaxy, though it is only several light weeks across (as opposed to the Milky Way, which is 100,000 light *years* across).

Radiation   Energy that is carried in waves. It includes electromagnetic energy and subatomic particles that are moving close to the speed of light.

Radio telescope   A directional radio antenna used in astronomy to detect and collect data on sources of radio waves in the cosmos. Penzias and Wilson used a radio telescope to discover the cosmic microwave background in 1964.

Recede   To move away from the observer (on Earth in most cases).

Redshift   An increase in the wavelength of light. This can arise from motion of the source or receiver (Doppler shift), from the expansion of space, or from strong gravitational fields.

Relative brightness   How bright one object is compared to another. If two objects have the same intrinsic brightness, their relative brightness tells us which one is closer, and by how much.

Relativistic Heavy Ion Collider (RHIC)   Located at New York's Brookhaven National Laboratory, the RHIC has reproduced the quark-gluon plasma by colliding gold nuclei.

Scatter   Describes what happens when an object absorbs light from one direction and then emits light in all directions. Daylight comes from a small point (the Sun), but on cloudy days it seems to come from all directions because of increased scattering.

Scientific method   A systematic way of looking at the world around us and solving its mysteries. It is a rigorous method for thinking and making observations, for building a case fact by fact, and for using evidence in a logical way.

Space-time   The combination of space and time into a four-dimensional Universe.

Spectral line   A line that appears in an otherwise uniform spectrum, at a specific frequency or wavelength. A spectral line shows either the emission of light, which makes a bright line, or the absorption of light, which leaves a dark line.

Spectrum   A range of possible measurements. In physics, a spectrum usually refers to all the different wavelengths or colors (if in the visible range) of light.

Standard candle   A celestial object whose intrinsic brightness is known or can be closely estimated. The observed brightness can help determine its distance.

Standard model   The description of fundamental particles and forces that has held up to the most vigorous scientific testing since the 1970s.

Steady state theory   A cosmological model that says the Universe has always been and will always be the same as it is now. The cosmic microwave background radiation has provided conclusive evidence against the steady state theory.

Strings   In theory, the most fundamental components of matter are not point-like subatomic particles. The particles themselves arise from the vibrations of tiny two-dimensional strings.

Strong force   The extremely strong but extremely short-range attractive force. It binds together the quarks and/or antiquarks to make hadrons, such as protons and neutrons. The leftover strong interactions keep the nucleus together.

Supermassive black hole   A black hole whose mass is on the order of between 10^5 and 10^{10} times the mass of the Sun. Scientists now think that most, if not all, galaxies, including the Milky Way, have supermassive black holes at their centers.

Supernova   An extremely bright explosion of a star at the end of its lifetime. Dying stars that grow too large may collapse in on themselves, or white dwarfs that get too heavy may trigger a thermonuclear explosion. The shock waves and expelled matter from supernovae are responsible for the birth of new stars.

Type Ia supernova   A supernova formed from the explosion of an old, compact star (white dwarf). Because of their uniform brightness, they make good standard candles.

Universe   All of space and time, along with all the matter and energy in it.

Variable stars   Stars that brighten and dim, some with precise timing. Cepheid variables have a period that allows us to determine their brightness, and from their brightness we can determine their distance.

Wavelength   The distance between two peaks of a wave. Usually designated by λ (lambda), it is the distance needed by a wave to make a complete oscillation. For visible light, this is on the order of 500 nanometers.

Bibliography

Burgess Cliff, and Fernando Quevedo. "The Great Cosmic Roller-Coaster Ride: Could Cosmic Inflation Be a Sign That Our Universe Is Embedded in A Far Vaster Realm?" *Scientific American* (October 2007): 52–61.

Carr, Joseph L. *The Art Of Science: A Practical Guide To Experiments, Observations, And Handling Data.* San Diego: HighText Publications, 1992.

Castelvecchi, Davide. "The Growth Of Inflation: Twenty-Five Years After Alan Guth Turned Cosmology on Its Head, What's The Latest Story of the Universe's First Moments?" *Symmetry Magazine* (December 2004/January 2005): 12–17.

Christianson, Gale E. *Edwin Hubble: Mariner of the Nebulae.* Chicago: University of Chicago Press, 1996.

Chui, Glennda. "The Great String Debate: Wisecracks Fly When Brian Greene and Lawrence Krauss Tangle Over String Theory." *Symmetry Magazine* (May 2007): 16–21.

Conselice, Christopher. "The Universe's Invisible Hand: Dark Energy Does More Than Hurry Along The Expansion Of The Universe. It Also Has a Stranglehold on the Shape and Spacing of Galaxies." *Scientific American* (February 2007): 34–41.

Folger, Tim. "The Big Bang Machine: A Long Island Particle Smasher Recreates the Moment of Creation." *Discover* (February 2007): 32–38.

Glanz, James. "Tests Suggest Scientists Have Found Big Bang Goo." *The New York Times* (January 14, 2004).

Kaufman, Marc. "Huge Black Holes May Hold Keys to Galaxy Formation." *The Washington Post* (October 31, 2007): A1.

Kolb, Rocky. *Blind Watchers of the Sky: The People and Ideas that Shaped our View of the Universe.* New York: Basic Books, 1996.

Kragh, Helge. *Cosmology and Controversy: The Historical Development of Two Theories of the Universe.* Princeton: Princeton University Press, 1996.

Linder, Eric. "On the Trail of Dark Energy." *CERN Courier* (September 4, 2003): 23.

May, Brian, Sir Patrick Moore, and Chris Lintott. *Bang! The Complete History of the Universe.* London: Carlton Books, 2006.

National Research Council, Committee on the Physics of the Universe, Michael S. Turner, chair. *Connecting Quarks With the Cosmos: Eleven Science Questions for the New Century.* Washington, D.C.: National Academy Press, 2002.

NSF-NASA-DOE Astronomy and Astrophysics Advisory Committee, and NSF-DOE High Energy Physics Advisory Panel, Edward W. Kolb, chair. *Report of the Dark Energy Task Force.* Washington, D.C.: National Science Foundation, 2006.

Perlmutter, Saul. "Supernovae, Dark Energy and the Accelerating Universe." *Physics Today,* (April 2003): 53–63.

Perricone, Mike. "The High-Energy Cosmic Mystery." *FermiNews* (April 16, 1999): 5–7.

Shackelford, Scott. "Worlds Without End: Marrying Particle Physics (the Study of the Very Small) to Cosmology (the Study Of the Very Large), André Linde Argues That Our Universe Is Just One of Many." *Stanford Magazine.* (November–December 2007): 56–62.

Singh, Simon. *Big Bang: The Origin of The Universe.* New York: HarperCollins, 2004.

Trefil, James S. *The Moment of Creation: Big Bang Physics from Before the First Millisecond to the Present Universe.* New York: Macmillan Publishing, 1983.

Veneziano, Gabriele. "The Myth of the Beginning of Time." *Scientific American* (May 2004): 54–65.

Weinberg, Steven. *The First Three Minutes: A Modern View of the Origin of The Universe.* New York: Bantam Books, 1983.

Further Resources

Abbott, Edwin A. *Flatland: A Romance of Many Dimensions.* New York: Barnes and Noble, 2004.

Gamow, George. *The New World of Mr. Tompkins.* Revised by Russell Stannard. Cambridge: Cambridge University Press, 2001.

Greene, Brian. *The Fabric of the Cosmos: Space, Time and the Texture of Reality.* New York: Vintage Books, 2004.

Guth, Alan H. *The Inflationary Universe: The Quest for a New Theory of Cosmic Origins.* New York: Perseus Books, 1997.

Hawking, Lucy and Stephen Hawking. *George's Secret Key to the Universe.* New York: Simon and Schuster, 2007.

Hawking , Stephen. *The Universe in a Nutshell.* New York: Bantam, 2001.

Hooper, Dan. *Dark Cosmos: In Search of our Universe's Missing Mass and Energy.* New York: HarperCollins, 2006.

Isaacson, Walter. *Einstein: His Life and Universe.* New York: Simon and Schuster, 2007.

Lederman, Leon, and David Schramm. *From Quarks to the Cosmos: Tools of Discovery.* New York: W.H. Freeman, 1995.

Lederman, Leon, with Dick Teresi. *The God Particle: If the Universe is the Answer, What is the Question?* New York: Delta, 1993.

Lincoln, Don. *Understanding the Universe: From Quarks to the Cosmos.* New York: World Scientific Publishing Company, 2004

Web sites

American Institute of Physics: Ideas of Cosmology
http://www.aip.org/history/cosmology/ideas/expanding.htm

Cosmic Background Explorer
http://lambda.gsfc.nasa.gov/product/cobe/

Fermilab
http://www.fnal.gov/

> *The Tevatron at Fermi National Accelerator Laboratory in Batavia, Illinois, was the site of the 1995 discovery of the top quark. This site contains explanations of particle physics, the science of matter, space and time ("Inquiring Minds"), and descriptions of projects and experiments ranging from particle collisions, to the production of antimatter, to the search for dark matter.*

Large Hadron Collider, CERN (European Organization for Nuclear Research)
http://public.web.cern.ch/Public/Welcome.html.

NASA
http://www.nasa.gov/

> *The National Aeronautics and Space Administration Web site offers a complete illustrated education on space exploration, from the Space Shuttle program and the Hubble Space Telescope, to the next generation of space telescopes and observatories, to the Beyond Einstein program, and on to just about any Universe-related topic you can imagine. The "For Students" link offers graded tutorials (Grades K–4, 5–8, 9–12 and Higher Education) for both students and educators. The many links include "Ask an Astrophysicist," and the Star Child learning center for young astronomers. There is even a section on "The Science of Star Trek."*

The Nobel Foundation
http://nobelprize.org/

> *With background for every Nobel Prize since 1901, the official site presents Nobel lectures, biographies, interviews, photos, articles, video clips, press releases, educational games, and a great deal more information about the Nobel laureates and their work.*

The Particle Adventure: The Fundamentals of Matter and Force
http://www.particleadventure.org/

> *The Particle Date Group of Lawrence Berkeley National Laboratory presents an interactive tour of quarks, neutrinos, antimatter, extra dimensions, dark matter, accelerators, and particle detectors.*

Relativistic Heavy Ion Collider, Brookhaven National Laboratory
http://www.bnl.gov/rhic/

Sloan Digital Sky Survey
http://www.sdss.org/

Super Nova Acceleration Probe, Lawrence Berkeley National Laboratory
http://snap.lbl.gov

The Universe Adventure
http://www.universeadventure.org/index.html
> *Also from Lawrence Berkeley National Laboratory, this site provides a complete and entertaining overview of cosmology, exploring the history, structure, and fate of the Universe. Segments include Fundamentals of Cosmology, Evidence for the Big Bang, Eras of the Cosmos, and Final Frontier.*

Wilkinson Microwave AnisotropyProbe
http://map.gsfc.nasa.gov/

Picture Credits

Index

About the Author

Mike Perricone writes about cosmology, astrophysics, and high-energy physics. He was a senior editor and science writer for nearly a decade in the Office of Public Affairs at Fermi National Accelerator Laboratory in Batavia, Illinois, working on the award-winning science periodicals *FermiNews* and *Symmetry*. His career as writer and reporter encompasses a lengthy stint as a sportswriter, including 12 years at *The Chicago Sun-Times*. Mike is also the author of *From Deadlines to Diapers: Journal of an At-Home Father* (Noble Press, Chicago, 1992). A member of the National Association of Science Writers, Mike lives with his family in historic Riverside, Ill. Mike would like to thank Professor Edward "Rocky" Kolb, chair of the Department of Astronomy and Astrophysics, Enrico Fermi Institute and the University of Chicago; and Ms. Jodi Bauer, science teacher at Hauser Junior High School in Riverside, Ill., for their invaluable help.